MW01155139

BLURRED TRANSPARENCIES IN CONTEMPORARY GLASS ARCHITECTURE

Blurred Transparencies in Contemporary Glass Architecture brings to light complex readings of transparent glass through close observations of six pivotal works of architecture. Written from the perspectives of a practitioner, the six essays challenge assumptions about fragility and visual transparency of glass.

A material imbued with idealism and utopic vision, glass has captured architects' imagination, and glass's fragility and difficulties in thermal control continue to present technical challenges. In recent decades, architecture has witnessed an emergence of technological advancements in chemical coating, structural engineering, and fabrication methods that have resulted in new kinds of glass transparencies. Buildings examined in the book include a sanatorium with expansive windows delivering light and air to recovering tuberculosis patients, a pavilion with a crystal clear glass plenum circulating air for heating and cooling, a glass monument symbolizing the screen of personal devices that shortened the distance between machines and humans, and a glass building symbolizing the social and material intertwining in the glass ceiling metaphor.

Connecting material glass to broader cultural and social contexts, *Blurred Transparencies in Contemporary Glass Architecture* enlightens students and practitioners of architecture as well as the general public with interest in design. The author demonstrates how glass is rarely crystal clear but is blurred both materially and metaphysically, revealing complex readings of ideas for which glass continues to stand.

Aki Ishida is Associate Professor of Architecture at Virginia Tech and a registered architect.

"This well-considered volume on glass is a pleasure to read for those of us who are fascinated by material exploration and detail. *Blurred Transparencies in Contemporary Glass Architecture* engages both academic and practicing architects and will certainly be required reading for both. I am asking all of my studio colleagues to read it."

– Julie Snow, Founding Design Principal,
Snow Kreilich Architects

"Aki Ishida's thoroughly researched and thoughtful *Blurred Transparencies in Contemporary Glass Architecture* reveals essential truths. It should serve as a clear demonstration of the importance of reflection and scholarship by practitioners, providing insights at the intersections of craft, technology, and history. As we struggle with the blurriness of transparency across our culture and society, such detailed and subtle insights into the physical construction of transparency provides not just these discoveries, but an essential window into the larger condition also."

– Nicholas de Monchaux, Craigslist Distinguished Chair in New
Media and Professor of Architecture and Urban Design,
University of California, Berkeley

"Any design student, and every design instructor, should read this book. In six historically grounded case studies Aki Ishida show how a presumably familiar material—glass—can, through manufacturing advances and novel design, remain a source of innovation, surprise, and discovery."

– Sandy Isenstadt, Professor of Modern Architecture,
University of Delaware

"Aki Ishida's investigations recall Bauhaus pedagogy where design emerges from the artistry of studying a substantive material. She choreographs physical qualities of glass alongside experiential gestalt, environmental systems beside a social milieu. *Blurred Transparencies in Contemporary Glass Architecture* is an essential read for a spectrum of design enthusiasts."

– Heather Woofter, Sam and Marilyn Fox Professor, Director of the
College of Architecture and Graduate School of Architecture &
Urban Design, Washington University in St. Louis

"Unique to Ishida's book is its capacity to interweave architectural history, cultural interpretation, building construction analysis and the acumen that can only come from first-hand observation of the buildings studied. A practicing architect, educator and installation artist working across fields, Ishida provides a comprehensive resume of glass architecture's development from the 19th century to the present, always set in relation to the history of its reception in the popular imagination and in scholarly studies. At the same time, she never neglects the building as physical artifact, with all its spatial, material and technical complexities. Her chosen case studies, ranging from canonical early 20th century buildings to more controversial recent projects in the US and Europe, integrate into a logical narrative all the aspects of glass architecture that a thinking architect, a critical student or a curious layperson would want to explore."

– Lynnette Widder, Lecturer in the Discipline of Sustainability Management,
Columbia University

"This book may be the most exciting exploration of cultural and social connotations and the architectural reading of glass as a modern building material since Paul Scheerbart's prophetical publication *Glasarchitektur* of 1914. It takes us from the clear-cut modernist perception of this diaphanous material to the multi-faceted appreciation of its transparency in recent years. A revealing book for architects and anyone who has an interest in the turbulent development of contemporary architecture."

– Wessel de Jonge, Architect, Professor of Heritage & Design,
Delft University of Technology, the Netherlands

BLURRED TRANSPARENCIES IN CONTEMPORARY GLASS ARCHITECTURE

Material, Culture, and Technology

Aki Ishida
Foreword by James Carpenter

Routledge
Taylor & Francis Group

NEW YORK AND LONDON

First published 2020
by Routledge
52 Vanderbilt Avenue, New York, NY 10017

and by Routledge
2 Park Square, Milton Park, Abingdon, Oxon, OX14 4RN

Routledge is an imprint of the Taylor & Francis Group, an informa business

© 2020 Taylor & Francis

The right of Aki Ishida to be identified as author of this work has
been asserted by her in accordance with sections 77 and 78 of the
Copyright, Designs and Patents Act 1988.

All rights reserved. No part of this book may be reprinted or
reproduced or utilised in any form or by any electronic, mechanical,
or other means, now known or hereafter invented, including
photocopying and recording, or in any information storage or retrieval
system, without permission in writing from the publishers.

Trademark notice: Product or corporate names may be trademarks or
registered trademarks, and are used only for identification and
explanation without intent to infringe.

Library of Congress Cataloging-in-Publication Data
Names: Ishida, Aki, author.
Title: Blurred transparencies in contemporary glass architecture :
material, culture, and technology / Aki Ishida.
Description: New York, NY : Routledge, 2020. | Includes
bibliographical references and index.
Identifiers: LCCN 2019049382 (print) | LCCN 2019049383 (ebook) |
ISBN 9781138584013 (hbk) | ISBN 9781138584020 (pbk) |
ISBN 9780429506284 (ebk)
Subjects: LCSH: Glass construction. | Transparency in architecture.
Classification: LCC NA4140 .I85 2020 (print) |
LCC NA4140 (ebook) | DDC 721/.04496–dc23
LC record available at https://lccn.loc.gov/2019049382
LC ebook record available at https://lccn.loc.gov/2019049383

ISBN: 978-1-138-58401-3 (hbk)
ISBN: 978-1-138-58402-0 (pbk)
ISBN: 978-0-429-50628-4 (ebk)

Typeset in Bembo
by Swales & Willis, Exeter, Devon, UK

Cover photograph: Iwan Baan (2007)

This book is dedicated to Takuzo Ishida (1944–2019)

CONTENTS

FIGURES

FOREWORD

James Carpenter

Blurred Transparencies, the title of Aki Ishida's book, opens up one of the greatest conflicts in terms of the definition of glass. We take the notion of transparency as a given with glass, yet we do not examine the term nor the material deeply enough to allow ourselves to "read" or "see" this material surface: a surface comprised of innumerable overlays of refraction, reflection, and transmission. Each of these optical fragments informs us of a complex simultaneity of events upon, within, and beyond, which make up our reality. It is as if "transparent glass" has somehow physically manifested and mediated the ancient philosophical conflict between "extramission" and "intromission."

Dating from the 5th century BC, theories of vision were the source of much debate among philosophers. On the one hand some philosophers believed in extramission, where emissions from the eyes "caused" perception by their interaction with the world, and on the other were those who argued that vision was the result of emissions from the world itself, "causing" perception in the eye. Over the centuries both ideas persisted, sometimes simultaneously.

Even as we now better understand the biology, chemistry, and physics of vision, the discourse between extramission and intromission is still useful when articulating the observation of glass materiality. The mutability of glass can easily be equated with its observation. By this I mean that it is as if our focused observation of glass changes the nature of its materiality. Where you may have seen only "transparency," you might now see the multiple interactions between reflection, refraction, and transmission, becoming more aware of the nature of light itself. By its range of examples and categorizations, Ishida's book aims to enliven our perception of glass and reminds us that the nature of glass, particularly in its relation to light, is not without mystery and ongoing scientific discovery.

Ishida worked in our studio for four years, starting in 1998, and participated in the realization of several projects. At that time, our studio had been leading the development of structural glass for over 20 years, while my own involvement with glass as a material began in 1968 and included a decade of consulting with Corning, specifically working with Dr. Donald Stookey, perhaps the most important glass chemist of the last century. During that period of time, working closely with Dr. Stookey on photosensitive glasses, my understanding of glass both technically and philosophically expanded to the point, where today, I understand glass as a material state, one which has an unlimited potential to achieve almost any conceivable end. For myself, it is the material of the future as much as it has been the material of the recent past.

With this in mind, Ishida's chapters each focus upon building examples utilizing different types of glasses appropriate to their time. These variables have to do with the means of manufacture and composition of the glass type in addition to secondary processes such as sophisticated coatings, where glass is an ideal substrate. The projects selected range from the most idealistic and socially responsible, to ones which are very much individualistic statements. In each, one can discern a shifting emphasis upon appropriate use of the material relative to engineering and outcome. Although today, intromission and extramission are not a philosophical or scientific point of debate, this book, and its exploration of glass in modern and contemporary architecture, makes clear that the conceptual framework afforded by glass and transparency remains a vital avenue for cultural and technological investigation.

PREFACE

My work with glass in architecture stems from over four years working at James Carpenter Design Associates in New York. Carpenter is a MacArthur "Genius Grant" Fellow with an international reputation for the design of advanced light-modulating glass structures. His mode of cross-disciplinary design research into the phenomena of light is a profound influence on, and the foundation for, my ongoing work and this book. Carpenter's studio often partners with architecture offices to design parts of buildings that required glass expertise and, at other times, experimented with new uses of glass in public art commissions. As a material that allows penetration of light and view, an understanding of glass is intrinsically linked to the study of light. At Carpenter's studio, I first observed my more experienced colleagues scrutinize glass samples under various light conditions, with a variety of materials and light sources in front of or behind the glass. We studied, specified, detailed, and tested mockups of a range of glass in buildings. Photographing glass samples and mockups became a means to capture light behaviors that our eyes might miss. I discovered that our eyes and mind can be trained to see phenomena, such as reflections and refractions of light, which deepen our understanding of materials. I quickly realized that glass is not simply glass.

The studio's work from the 1970s led research in the structural use of glass and this directly influenced many engineers and fabricators specializing in today's structural glass and glass constructions. Together, designers and engineers came to understand elusive material intimately from experience, expanded possibilities of design with glass, and bolstered our confidence in pushing the limits of glass. It took some years afterward to realize that the four and a half years I spent at Carpenter's studio – from 1998 to 2002 – occurred during a pivotal moment in architectural uses of glass. Some significant applications, including bullet- and hurricane-resistant ionoplast interlayer to fabricate structural glass stair treads and walls, North America's first completion of cable net glass walls engineered by Schlaich Bergermann Partner, and lamination of metal hardware between sheets of glass, were realized in this relatively short period. These projects altered the perception of glass as a structural material. Around this time, types of glass finishes that were only exclusively known or access-ible in architectural practices – including acid etched, patterned, fritted, and lamin-ated with graphic-printed interlayers or metal mesh – became more widely available and specified. One could say that this period, around 2000, was a turning point in glass architecture, and certainly was in my architecture career.

This background in glass, combined with a number of years at the offices of Rafael Viñoly Architects, I. M. Pei Architects, and at my own, became a foundation for my full-time academic position at Virginia Tech. Since my first year in 2012, I have taught undergraduate design studios and Building Materials, a lecture class for sophomores. The course is the first in the sequence of four building technology courses required for an undergraduate professional degree in architecture. My pedagogy relies on a combination of lectures and hands-on projects that ask the students to examine the properties of each material, such as casting concrete blocks and photographing glass samples under varying light conditions. Learning about materials from experience is combined with readings on both factual properties and theoretical inquiries. The Building Materials course made an important revelation to me about architects' education. I observed that the students are introduced to historical notions of transparency in history and theory classes and, separately in building technology courses, to the art of window or curtain wall detailing. The discon-nect between theory and practice is rooted in our education. Furthermore, in design studios, investigations into the materiality of glass are often limited to its see-through quality. Glass is rarely modeled as anything more than a clear acrylic sheet, or represented in drawings as a shiny surface. In fact, glass is often represented as an absence of material; window frames are modeled with no infill to represent glass, utterly omitting a defining phenomenon of glass: reflections. Even though I also received my architectural education in the same way a couple of decades ago, I found myself confounded by the binary separ-ation between theory and practice in learning about building materials.

It took a few years of full-time academic career to comprehensively reflect upon and link what I learned in history and theory courses to my experience of investigating glass as a practitioner. This book is, therefore, neither a technical handbook on how to detail glass construction, nor a book written by a historian with a PhD in architecture. Instead, it is a book that reflects upon the rich, multi-various contexts of glass, written from the point of a practitioner. I wrote the book with students, academics, and practitioners in mind, with the hope that it may deepen and broaden their understanding of glass and transparency and, conse-quently, expand their imagination to ask new questions and to seek new applica-tions for glass in their buildings.

ACKNOWLEDGMENTS

There are many who have influenced and encouraged my investigations into the transparency of glass. I am indebted to my mentor and former employer James Carpenter for sparking my interest in light and glass early in my career. From Jamie and the colleagues in his studio (in particular, Richard Kress, Luke Lowings, and Marek Walczak), I learned that glass is never simply glass, and that the atmospheric effects of glass and the technical specification and details are inseparable. I gained knowledge that comes from the direct observation of materials, and this approach to research and design continues to influence my own work and teaching today.

I am grateful to my mentors, peers, and former students for their editorial input and encouragement at various stages in the past two and a half years. These people include Paul Emmons, Frank Weiner, Davidson Norris, Lynnette Widder, Peter Pelsinski, Alexander Bala, Joseph Bedford, Bill Green, Matthew Wisnioski, Helene Renard, Hayley Owens, Cynthia Jara, Reid Freeman, and others who supported me along the way.

I am very fortunate to have had the support of Jennifer Lawrence, the director of the Writing Center at the Newman Library of Virginia Tech. Over three semesters, she kept me writing almost daily regardless of my other deadlines, distractions, or shifting temperaments. You are my trusted personal coach in writing, and more. Peter Potter, the director of publishing strategy at Virginia Tech, guided me through contract negotiation. I am thankful for the research help of my diligent graduate assistants Shubham Chuhadia and Qianru Lai.

At Routledge, I thank the editors Katharine Maller and Krystal LaDuc, for their insights and encouragement, and editorial assistant Julia Pollacco for shepherding the book's production.

Interviews with people who have direct experience with each of the six buildings were particularly critical to the development of my book. I am also indebted to the patient assistance of people at various archives who provided primary sources for my research.

For Zonnestraal Sanatorium, I am grateful to Wessel de Jonge, one of the architects who skillfully restored Zonnestraal and leads the Heritage and Architecture Studios at Delft University of Technology, for his generous gift of time and firsthand expertise. Jan Schriefer, who grew up at Zonnestraal with his father who was a recovering tuberculosis patient, gave two memorable tours of the buildings and the ground. His stories brought to light the lasting impact of the sanatorium on the individual souls of those who lived there. Joppe Schaaper, Tobias van der Knaap, and others at the International Institute of Social History in Amsterdam helped me obtain historic drawings and photographs, as did Iris de Jong and Herman Gelton of the Het Nieuwe Instituut archive.

For the Willis Building, I thank the building manager Peter Page and Vicki Chapman of Willis Towers Watson in Ispwich for hosting an informative visit to the building. Alicia Valdivieso Royo at the Norman Foster Foundation patiently responded to my multiple requests for drawings and photographs.

For the Javits Center and the glass ceiling chapter, I am delighted to have interviewed Marilyn Loden, the woman who popularized the phrase "glass ceiling" in 1978. Perry Chin, a project architect for the Javits Center, provided firsthand knowledge of working with I. M. Pei and James Ingo Freed. Emma Cobb at the office of Pei Cobb Freed & Partners assisted me in searching for photographs and drawings.

For the Glass Pavilion in Toledo, I am grateful to Toshihiro Oki, project architect for SANAA, and Na Min Mike Ra of façade consultant Front for the illuminating phone interviews. The office of SANAA was exceptionally swift and generous in providing drawings. Ashley Wilson of the National Trust for Historic Preservation provided detailed specifications of glass at both the Glass House by Philip Johnson and the Farnsworth House by Mies.

For Apple's 5th Avenue cube, I thank Karl Backus at Bohlin Cywinski Jackson for a generous interview and invaluable stories on his experience working with Steve Jobs and Apple, and Karen Robichaud at BCJ for searching for the photographs. I also had the fortune of consulting with my former collaborators and experts in the field of highly specialized glass architecture: James O'Callaghan of Eckersley O'Callaghan, the lead glass engineer on the Apple cube and stairs, and Michael Mulhern of TriPyramid Structures, the fabricator of the metal fittings.

For Harpa, Sigurður Einarsson of Batteríið Architects gave me an informative tour of the building, and Studio Olafur Eliasson was generous in sharing photographs. Through the Akademie der Künste in Berlin, I was able to obtain drawings of visionary glass architecture by Bruno Taut.

Although the drive for the book is sustained by passion for architecture and scholarship, passion alone is not sufficient for the execution of a book. I thank the School of Architecture + Design at Virginia Tech for the resources that enabled my trips to study buildings in Hilversum, Ipswich, Reykjavik, and New York. Reproduction and copyrights for the images in the book were funded by Virginia Tech's Faculty Book Publishing Subvention Fund, which combines contributions from four entities at the university: the School of Architecture + Design, the College of Architecture and Urban Studies, the Office of the Provost, and the University Libraries.

Last, this book is dedicated to my late father Takuzo Ishida whom we lost to cancer as I completed the last chapters of this book. He was a research chemist and a connoisseur of the arts. The coexistence of science and art in our lives since childhood undoubtedly fueled my fascination with the synthesis of art and technology in architecture. He instilled in me the curiosity, conviction, and self-discipline necessary to begin and complete this book and, for that, I am eternally grateful.

Blacksburg, Virginia, 2019

1

INTRODUCTION

Glass

A material that is neither liquid nor solid, glass is amorphous, hovering between the two states. In a near-magical process, ordinary sand is transformed into a fragile, see-through material. This transformative nature of glass has captured people's imagination throughout history. From the 11th to the 16th century, the secrets of glassmaking were highly coveted by the Venetians, until three glass-makers were smuggled in by King Louis XIV of France for Versailles Hall of Mir-rors. Glass's historical exclusivity continues to impact metaphors associated with glass today. Crystals, glass, and mirrors appear symbolically in literature, art, and architecture, both religious and secular. Art historian Rosemarie Haag Bletter traces the history of glass as a metaphor of transformation in society, from the tales of King Solomon and the Renaissance *Dream of Poliphilo* to German Expressionism and Bauhaus.[1] Glass slippers, coffins, and mirrors often appear symbolically in fairy tales, which describe the collective dreams of a culture. In modern architecture, glass is a material imbued with idealism, symbolism, and utopic vision.[2] Glass's fragility, which intensifies its exquisiteness, along with difficulties in thermal control, have challenged architects over the past century. As Bletter writes, because of glass's preciousness in preindustrial periods, coupled with its brittleness, glass appeared frequently in architectural fantasies – in the "realm of wishful thinking."[3] Glass is physically heavy, but metaphysically light. Together, these are the basis of the paradoxical allure of glass.

Glass, in a seemingly multivalent contradiction, combines immaterial qualities with material properties. Following an accelerated development in materials and glass engineering in the past few decades, knowledge about both spatial effects and technical performance of glass has greatly expanded. In this time period,

FIGURE 1.1 A drawing from the book *Alpine Architecture* by Bruno Taut. Glass architecture built on Monte Generoso gives the effect of glass mosaic.

Akademie der Künste, Berlin, Alpine Architektur aus dem Bruno-Taut-Archiv Nr. 21.

architecture has witnessed an emergence of technical advancements – including chemical coatings that alter reflective and refractive properties, plastic lamination interlayers that give structural stiffness to glass panels, and fabrication techniques that allow precision machined hardware to become embedded in glass. Consequently, structures that could only be drawn or written about previously, including those by prophetic poet Paul Scheerbart and the visionary architect Bruno Taut (Figure 1.1), have now been realized. As material properties are altered, they, in turn, call into question the prevailing social and cultural symbolisms and metaphors associated with glass. It is necessary, therefore, to reconsider glass transparency in the context of recent developments and cultural changes. The prevailing perceptions of glass have become blurred, both materially and metaphysically.

Transparency

Transparency is both fundamental and elusive. In architecture, its metaphorical meanings are as multivalent and mutable as the visual effects of glass, varying temporally and spatially. The medieval Latin root of the English word transparent is *transparare*, meaning "shining through."[4] The Renaissance architect Filarete, among others, describes transparent materials like glass as "diaphanous," a word with a Greek origin meaning to "show through." The Japanese word for transparency is 透明 (tōmei). The character 透 means to permeate, and 明 is brightness or clarity. Physics explains that when light passes through a transparent material, it slows down, giving it a shimmering quality. Light passing through a diamond travels about half as fast as it does in a vacuum – but still at over 86,000 mps.[5] This material quality gives glass a nearly magical significance that has been noted for centuries and led to the widespread theory that transparent objects capture and hold light within themselves, as if beacons.[6] In this way, glass enters the imagination as a materialization of light, a substantial spirituality.

Blurring of Transparency

To blur means to make the difference between two things less clear. When a night sky is photographed in long exposure, the earth's rotation causes motion blur, an apparent streaking that resembles arched star trails. In optics, the blurring of an image is related to the depth of field. When the human eye looks at an object, the object in focus appears sharp on the retina, but objects in front or behind appear blurred. As the focal plane moves within the depth of field, so do the areas that are less focused. In other words, blurring is relational and mutable. In architecture, when glass is experienced in motion under changing light, the perception of it is not simply as transparent but is a specific kind of transparency that can be called blurred. As new techniques in glass-making have expanded the range of effects and performance of clear glass, its transparency is increasingly multivalent and complex, making nuanced differences difficult to perceive. As the perception of material becomes more blurred, the prevailing cultural and social meanings associated with glass are also blurred.

While differences between translucent – frosted glass and perforated materials that filter light and view – and clear glass are easy to discern visually, different types of clear glass are not casually distinguishable by sight, even if they possess strikingly different structural and physical properties, such as stiffness or resistance to breakage. What may be indiscernible to the eye can have a substantial impact on the overall appearance and performance of a glass building, that, in turn, impacts one's experience and challenges prevailing meanings associated with glass. These properties can enable spatial effects and performance that were previously unobtainable and, consequently, not fully included in architectural discourse. For example, two sheets of glass, which may look identical on first glance, can behave entirely differently in how they reflect or transmit light, or how they break. Innovative approaches to heating and cooling glass buildings have resulted in optically clear buildings that are relatively energy efficient, which contradicts the prevailing reputation of glass as an energy inefficient material.

Material properties, as well as specific light conditions, inevitably blur the transparency of even the clearest and cleanest glass. Transparency is always relative, and must be considered relative to light. If color, according to Josef Albers, is the most relative medium in art,[7] then transparency may be the most relative phenomena in architecture. In his 1935 essay "Glass, the Fundamental Material of Modern Architecture," Le Corbusier recognized the role of light in both poetic and technical realms of glass architecture: "The lyricism that attaches to light, whether sunlight or artificial light, is always an important element to consider in relation to architecture. The stage is set for poets, just as it is for technicians."[8]

The angle, luminance, and intensity of light that shines through a material transforms – or blurs – the perception of transparency; this is why the same glass building can have an entirely contrasting appearance depending on the light and the time of day. Study of the day–night cycle is critical to understanding the mutability of transparency. Moreover, electric light in nighttime architecture has altered what is seen on and through glass and deserves further consideration in addition to daylight.

Examination of Glass Transparency in Recent History

Despite its ubiquitous presence in contemporary architecture, glass transparency has seldom been examined deeply. Colin Rowe and Robert Slutzky's 1963 classic essay "Transparency: Literal and Phenomenal" remains a tenet of architectural thought.[9,10] Rowe and Slutzky consider the perceptual and compositional potential of transparency in painting and architecture but assume, rather than examine, its relation to materiality, specifically to glass. They define material transparency of glass as literal transparency, which they dismiss as unambiguous and limited in interpretations. Over time, the limitations of their binary understanding of transparency have been critically questioned.[11,12,13] The *Light Construction* exhibition of 1995, curated by Terence Riley at the Museum of Modern Art, investigated "the nature and potentials of architectural surfaces."[14] The survey of 30 projects notably brought attention to the extensive use of translucency in contemporary architecture. Concerned not only with the materials but the meanings they convey, the exhibit suggested that translucent materials become a veil that distance the viewer from the object. In 2007, Columbia University organized a multidisciplinary symposium on glass in architecture, entitled *Engineered Transparency*.[15] The event and the accompanying publication spawned discourse around the impact of engineering and fabrication technologies on glass architecture.

The Book's Approach

In order to deepen and broaden readings of glass transparency, *Blurred Transparencies* explores the interweaving of the historical, theoretical, and cultural aspects of glass buildings along with the practical. Practitioners' everyday concerns guide the chapters as well: technical details, material specification, structural and mechanical systems, budget, and constraints placed by the client. This book brings to light the complexities in the transparency of glass through close observations of six pivotal works of architecture, one modern and five contemporary. All are built with optically clear glass – not diffused or textured, which are in some ways inherently blurred – for their exceptional effects, which allows the focus to be on the qualities of transparency and reflectivity in glass. Each building has been selected to demonstrate how its glassy qualities transcend transparency as it has been understood in the discourse of modern architecture. Each chapter examines glass's physical properties and assembly details, interwoven with an intricate web of social and cultural metaphors and historic precedents. The book is neither a comprehensive documentation of glass architecture – which Michael Wigginton has done masterfully – nor a theoretical examination of glass architecture situated in a particular city and time – such as Annette Fierro on François Mitterand's *Grands Projets* in Paris,[16] Deborah Ascher Barnstone on postwar Germany,[17] or Isobel Armstrong on Victorian glass.[18] Instead, *Blurred Transparencies* is written through the lens of a practitioner-academic, interweaving the historical and cultural with practical and empirical knowledge in the architectural uses of glass. The book demonstrates how transparent glass is rarely crystal clear, but is blurred both materially and metaphysically, exploring complex ideas for which glass continues to stand.

Six Buildings

1. Matter Infused with Spirit: Zonnestraal Sanatorium's Healing Glass Transparency

Designed by Jan Duiker and Bernard Bijvoet in Hilversum, the Netherlands, Zonnestraal Sanatorium (1931) was built as an aftercare colony for tuberculosis patients. It was built in accordance with a Dutch functionalism principal that architecture can fulfill a spiritual role beyond practical functions. Its physical and metaphysical lightness is underscored by the delicacy of glass membrane on thin steel frames, which wrapped the building like a drapery. These expansive windows brought in light, fresh air, and views of the surroundings to heal the recovering patients. Built with nearly colorless single-lite drawn glass, Zonnestraal serves as a baseline to gauge how contemporary glass buildings have become less crystal clear and more blurred. During the judicious restoration of the building in the early 2000s, the original glass was replaced with a combination of single- and double-glazed glass to meet the standards of current thermal comfort. Comparisons between the original glass sheet and the contemporary glass assembly offer an opportunity to study how the perception of glass changes over time.

2. Mirroring Ipswich: Contextual Glass Transparency of the Willis Building

Willis Faber and Dumas Headquarters (1975) by Foster & Associates in Ipswich, UK made pioneering contributions to glass curtain wall buildings and the culture of workspaces. It blurred – or made less clear – the boundaries between the exterior and interior with reflective, frameless curtain walls. By suspending dark gray tinted and coated glass panels from concrete floors with metal corner patch plates, the faceted glass panels trace the irregularly curved streets of the medieval English town. In the daytime, the frameless glass becomes a scrim on which the masonry buildings across the intersection appear reflected and distorted. At night, the view on the façade is reversed: the transparent glass walls expose the illuminated interior like an X-ray. Additionally, with its expansive floor-to-ceiling glass walls, the Willis Building cultivated a new type of transparent landscape office architecture.

3. Cracking the Glass Ceiling of a Cystal Palace: The Jacob K. Javits Convention Center

On the days leading to the presidential election of 2016, many expected Hillary Clinton to claim her victory under the largest glass ceiling in New York City, the Jacob K. Javits Convention Center. The building was appropriated by the Clinton campaign as a symbol of a glass ceiling, the invisible barrier that stands between women and their career aspirations. Although Clinton's breaking of the glass ceiling was highly anticipated, she was able only to crack it. Ironically, as more women aspire to break the metaphorical glass ceiling, as a result of advancements in glass technology, glass has become harder to shatter. Historically, glass has been perceived as fragile. However, in the recent decades, incremental development in processes such as tempering, chemical strengthening, and lamination with plastic interlayers have made glass less prone to breakage. Consequently, changes in material property suggest that meanings of social and cultural metaphors have become blurred. This chapter examines the intertwining of technological developments, material properties, and cultural metaphors historically ascribed to materials.

4. Air, Light, and Liquid in Motion: The Glass Pavilion in Toledo

The Glass Pavilion (2006) by SANAA was conceived as an annex to the Toledo Museum of Art to house glass objects and glassblowing demonstrations. A single-story structure located in a park among trees, each space of the Pavilion is enclosed by a curved, transparent low-iron glass wall, described by Ryue Nishizawa as a "single stroke of [the] brush."[19] The effects seen on glass are watery and airy. As if watching a movie, glass objects, landscape, and molten glass are seen through layers of the curved glass walls, overlapped with flickering reflections of the surroundings. Through the interstitial spaces in between the clear glass enclosures, cooled and hot air is circulated into galleries, hallways, and demonstration shops. These crystal clear buffer zones visually connect the bubble-like glass rooms while thermally isolating them from each other. Steel columns and plumbing pipes are concealed within a few opaque gypsum walls, and the beams and girders are hidden above the ceilings. This concealment allows the massive, curved glass sheets to wind through the building like transparent ribbons with minimal obstructions. In these ways, the building is simultaneously both opaque and transparent, blurring the conventional distinction between spaces that are exhibited openly, with those concealed in an opaque *poché*.

5. Impermanent Monument for Intimate Machines: Apple's Glass Cube

Glass as a material has become fundamentally linked with Apple's products and architecture, ranging from its touch screens – the intimate medium through which most personal news and images are exchanged – to emblematic structural glass stairs in its flagship stores. Manhattan's 5th Avenue Apple Store's all-glass cube (2006) is a monument made of glass. The cube, while possessing characteristics of traditional monuments, blurs the prevailing notions of a monument by using the most advanced glass technologies of the time. Counter to the traditional monuments built with permanent, opaque materials, the cube is nearly all glass, a material perceived as fragile and impermanent. The cube's glass walls and roof, which are laminated with hurricane- and bullet-resistant ionoplast interlayers, serve both as the structure and the enclosure. Further underscoring its monumentality, the glass cube has been, since the store's opening in 2006, ritualistically reconstructed three times with the most current glass technologies, then ceremoniously revealed to display its technical prowess, as if it were the launch of a new Apple product. The cube is a profoundly effective symbol – a monument – for a company that has shortened the distance between humans and machines through a glass interface.

6. Quasi-Transparency of Harpa Concert Hall and Conference Centre

Harpa Concert Hall and Conference Centre (2011) in Reykjavik is characterized by the play of light on the crystal-like steel and glass polygonal façade comprising a steel frame and transparent glass infill. The 12-sided polygonal module, which serves as both the skin and the structure, has been described by its façade designer Olafur Eliasson as "quasi brick," suggesting heaviness of stacked masonry even though it is sheathed in light-transmitting glass. Stemming from the Latin word *quasi*, meaning "as if, almost," quasi is relational and changeable. The word characterizes not only this curious polyhedral façade, but also the physically and metaphysically multifaceted qualities of the glass building as a whole. Eliasson's inspiration for the building was the kaleidoscope, a toy that dissolves and reorganizes a view with a slight shift of the tube. Likewise, with a slight shift in the viewer's body, Harpa blurs, or continuously reconfigures, fragmented views of the city and the interior; it shows the world less clearly and blurs its transparency.

Each of the buildings studied or celebrated in these chapters is the product of collaborative effort to generate new kinds of glass transparency. Teams often unexpectedly engaged members from outside the discipline of architecture, such as a yacht designer (for the Willis Building) or an aircraft manufacturer (for the Apple glass cube). These stories suggest that, contrary to the predominant image of a singular master architect, new architectural possibilities are a result of teamwork. Building upon experiences from prior projects, experts from multiple disciplines mutually reinforce confidence in each other to push the technical limits of glass. In turn, technical advancements in glass architecture offer ways to challenge prevailing architectural meanings, social metaphors, and cultural symbolism associated with glass.

Notes

1 Rosemarie Haag Bletter, "Interpretation of Glass Dream: Expressionist Architecture and the History of the Crystal Metaphor," *Journal of the Society of Architectural Historians* 40, no. 1 (March, 1981) 20–43.

2 Ufuk Ersoy, "To See Daydreams: The Glass Utopia of Paul Scheerbart and Bruno Taut" in Nathaniel Coleman, Ed., *Imagining and Making the World: Reconsidering Architecture and Utopia* (New York: Peter Lang, 2011) 107–138.

3 Bletter, 22.

4 *Oxford Dictionaries*, *s.v.* "Transparent," accessed July 5, 2019, www.oxforddiction aries.com/definition/english/transparent.

5 Robert Hazen, "What Makes Diamond Sparkle?" *NOVA*, February 1, 2000, accessed August 26, 2019, www.pbs.org/wgbh/nova/article/diamond-science.

6 Emmons suggests that it was this perception that led to the still-prevalent cartoon representation of glass as a series of parallel diagonal lines of differing lengths. Paul Emmons, *Drawing Imagining Building: Embodiment in Architectural Drawing Practices* (Abingdon: Routledge, 2019), 147–149.

7 Josef Albers, *Interaction of Color* (New Haven, CT: Yale University Press, 2013).

8 Le Corbusier, Paul Stirton, and Tim Benton, "Glass, the Fundamental Material of Modern Architecture," *West 86th: A Journal of Decorative Arts, Design History, and Material Culture* 19, no. 2 (Fall–Winter, 2012), 306.

9 Colin Rowe and Robert Slutzky, "Transparency: Literal and Phenomenal," *Perspecta* 8 (1963), 45–54.

10 Colin Rowe and Robert Slutzky, *Transparency: With a Commentary by Bernhard Hoesli and an Introduction by Werner Oechslin* (Basel: Birkhäuser Verlag, 1997).

11 Rosemarie Haag Bletter, "Opaque Transparency," *Oppositions* 13 (Summer, 1978), 121–126.

12 Detlef Mertins, "Anything but Literal: Sigfried Giedion and the Reception of Cubism in Germany" in Detlef Mertins, Ed., *Modernity Unbound: Other Histories of Architectural Modernity* (London: Architectural Association, 2011) 24–69.

13 Emmanuel Petit. ed. *Reckoning with Colin Rowe: Ten Architects Take Position* (New York: Routledge, 2015).

14 Terence Riley, *Light Construction* (New York: Museum of Modern Art, 2004).

15 The symposium was chaired by Michael Bell, as one in a series of the Columbia Conference on Architecture, Engineering, and Materials, a multi-year research program hosted at Columbia University's Graduate School of Architecture, Planning and Preservation (GSAPP) in coordination with Columbia's Fu Foundation School of Engineering and Applied Science and the Institute for Lightweight Structures and Conceptual Design (ILEK) at the University of Stuttgart. Michael Bell and Jeannie Kim, *Engineered Transparency: The Technical, Visual, and Spatial Effects of Glass* (New York: Columbia GSAPP and Princeton Architectural Press, 2009).

16 Annette Fierro, *The Glass State: The Technology of the Spectacle, Paris, 1981–1998* (Cambridge, MA: MIT Press, 2003).

17 Deborah Ascher Barnstone, *The Transparent State: Architecture and Politics in Postwar Germany* (Abingdon: Routledge, 2005).

18 Isobel Armstrong, *Victorian Glassworlds: Glass Culture and the Imagination 1830–1880* (Oxford: Oxford University Press, 2008).

19 Kazuyo Sejima, Yukio Futagawa, and Ryue Nishizawa, *Kazuyo Sejima, Ryue Nishizawa 2006–2011* (Tokyo: A.D.A. Edita, 2011), 23.

2

MATTER INFUSED WITH SPIRIT
Zonnestraal Sanatorium's Healing Glass Transparency

An exemplar of modern glass architecture, Sanatorium Zonnestraal (Figure 2.1), completed in 1928 near Hilversum in the Netherlands, was built as an aftercare colony for tuberculosis patients. The recovery rooms spread out into the forests like rays of the sun (Figures 2.2 and 2.3); the expansive windows brought in light, fresh air, and views of the surrounding forest to the recovering patients. The design was conceived between 1925 and 1927 by Dutch architects Jan Duiker and Bernard Bijvoet, with structural engineer Jan Gerko Wiebenga. The design of Zonnestraal exemplifies *Het Nieuwe Bouwen*, a Dutch thread of functionalism, which asserts that matter is infused with spirit, and that architecture can fulfill a spiritual role beyond practical functions. Zonnestraal's lyricism and poetry underscore Duiker and Bijvoet's commitment to the spiritual powers of healing architecture. The architect and client anticipated eradication of tuberculosis within the next few decades, and intended Zonnestraal to be demolished when a cure was found.[1] Having accepted such an impermanent nature of the building, the architects designed the structure with a minimum amount of materials, using experimental, thin, reinforced concrete construction.[2] Its lightness and delicacy was further underscored by the single-lite, crystal clear glass membrane on thin steel frames, which wrapped the building like a drapery. Such dematerialization of steel, concrete, and glass resulted in an astonishingly delicate transparency that distinguishes this early modern glass building. As accurately predicted, the invention of triple drug therapy in the 1950s rendered tuberculosis sanatoria obsolete.[3] Zonnestraal's renovation over the subsequent five decades reveals that glass transparency is dependent on material properties and details specific to its time.

Certain Dutch ideologies and construction technologies of the 1920s profoundly influenced and shaped the use of glass at Zonnestraal. Of the six glass buildings examined in this book, Zonnestraal – despite being built before World

FIGURE 2.1 Sanatorium Zonnestraal after the 2001 restoration. Lightness and delicacy of thin reinforced concrete structure is underscored by single-lite glass that wraps the building like a drapery.

Photograph: Michel Kievits/Sybolt Voeten (2003).

FIGURE 2.2 Aerial view of Zonnestraal shows long, linear fingers that reach out to the landscape for exposure to light and air.

Photograph: Foto Aviodrome Lelystad (1931).

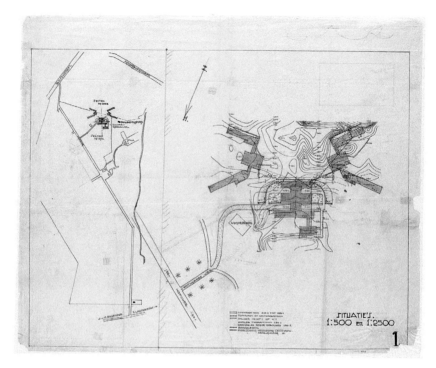

FIGURE 2.3 Duiker's site plan of the sanatorium on the estate. North arrow points downward (undated).

Het Nieuwe Instituut / DUDO collection, inv.nr.

War II – is most closely associated with principles of orthodox modern architecture. To understand the plurivalence of glass transparencies in the century that followed, the glazing of Zonnestraal – with its single-lite, low-iron glass with no coating or insulation – serves as a parameter to gauge how readings of contemporary glass buildings have become less crystal clear and more blurred. Zonnestraal echoes particular social and technical forces of the time and place in which it was designed: the nascent glass, steel, and concrete construction technologies on one hand and, on the other, the architects' anti-bourgeois thoughts associated with transparent buildings in 1920s' and 30s' Europe. Although architects of this period across Europe were greatly interested in symbolism associated with glass, Zonnestraal's transparency was shaped by ideologies of a specific thread of Dutch modernism. Additionally, the restoration of Zonnestraal's main building in 2003, which deftly combines the original curtain wall's delicacy with the thermal performance of today's insulated glass, further exhibits how Zonnestraal's glass transparency reflects its time, both physically and metaphysically.

Zonnestraal, a 20th Century Sanatorium

The sanatorium building type was established between the mid-1800s and the mid-1900s to isolate patients with contagious diseases from the community. An illness associated with industrialization and spread through breathing air contaminated with bacteria, tuberculosis mainly affected young, working-age urban dwellers, whose debilitation from the disease considerably impacted the workforce.[4] Since the cause of the disease was linked with unsanitary, crowded housing and workplaces, architects considered this epidemic crisis an architectural problem with a solution in hygienic architecture. Research into tuberculous treatment coincided with the advent of modernism in architecture; namely, modern buildings with expansive glass windows and flat roofs became a means to deliver fresh air and light to aid patients' recovery.[5] The sanatorium movement flourished in the Swiss Alps, based on the German Romantic belief in the healing power of mountains and the dry, cool alpine air. Davos, Switzerland became a place of healing for the wealthy, and patients came from all over the world. Thomas Mann's 1924 novel *The Magic Mountain* is a story of a man's treatment for tuberculosis at a Swiss sanatorium, based on the author's observations during his wife's stay at the Waldsanatorium in Davos. The Paimio Sanatorium (1932) in Finland by Alvar Aalto[6] and the Zonnestraal are two well-known exceptions built on flat land.[7] Zonnestraal is an early exemplar that directly translates the prevailing treatment for tuberculosis to an architecture designed for exposure to light and air through expansive windows and balconies.

In the 1910s, the diamond polishing industry in Amsterdam employed over ten thousand people, many of whom contracted tuberculosis from breathing diamond dust. The Dutch Diamond Workers' Union raised funds by selling copper waste from copper wire ends that held diamonds during cutting and diamond powder collected from the workers' overalls.[8] The union chose a site on a 286-acre woodland estate 40 minutes from Amsterdam. Duiker worked with limited funds raised by the diamond union. Zonnestraal consists of a central service building from which two detached pairs of residential pavilions (Figure 2.4) extend into the woods. Each of the two pavilions, of which only one was initially completed in 1928 together with the main building, has two linear, double-story wings set at a 45-degree angle to each other, so the view and light to each room could be maximized.[9] The radial plan intimates the name Zonnestraal, meaning "sunbeam" in Dutch. Rays of the sun, or a sparkling diamond, can also be discerned in the shimmering sunlight caught in the ripples of the drawn glass in the long ribbon windows.[10] These metaphors aligned closely with a widespread interest in crystal metaphors, glass, and light in modern architecture of the 1910s and 1920s, including Bruno Taut's Glass Pavilion (1914), Paul Scheerbart's book *Glasarchitektur* (1914),[11] and Walter Gropius's Bauhaus Building (1926). Gropius references the crystal symbol in the Bauhaus's opening manifesto, that "the new structure of the future ... will one day rise toward heaven from the hands of a million workers

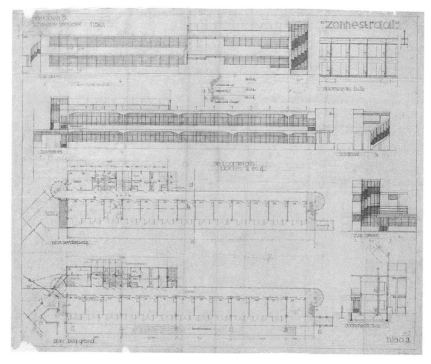

FIGURE 2.4 Duiker's design drawing for the Dresselhuys Pavilion. Ground floor plan, section, and elevation (1931).

Het Nieuwe Instituut/DUDO collection, inv. nr.

like the crystal symbol of a new faith."[12] The crystalline metaphor of this period stood for personal transformation and political metamorphosis.[13] At Zonnestraal, the sun transmitting through the glass walls would heal the sick patients, transforming them to healthy workers who could return to the workforce.

Zonnestraal's central building is arranged with several programmatic functions clustered around two vehicular passages (Figures 2.5 and 2.6), reminiscent of Villa Savoye, to loop through the ground floor; the kitchen and boiler room are located in a wing separated from the administrative and medical space. This layout results in an east–west axis that connects the sanatorium to the outside world. In contrast, the north–south axis ties the main building with the dining hall on the upper floor, through the open field, to the pavilions where the patients slept; this axis organized the daily rituals of patients recovering from a life-threatening disease. With this cross-axial layout, Duiker symbolically and poetically intersected patients' daily passages with the artery that tied the protected inner world of Zonnnestraal to the outside.[14]

FIGURE 2.5 Vehicular passage reminiscent of Villa Savoye loops through the ground floor of the main building.

Photograph: Author (2018).

New Dutch Architecture

The transparency of Zonnestraal's glass is closely intertwined with the ideologies behind *Het Nieuwe Bouwen* ("New Building"), a Dutch thread of the international functionalist movement of the early 1900s.[15] The polemics of *Het Nieuwe Bouwen* were decidedly anti-bourgeois, as evident in their concerns for housing designs for the working class.[16] At the same time, *Het Nieuwe Bouwen* had an undeniable aesthetic agenda, which was as influential as its fulfillment of functions. In fact, many critics and architects were drawn to *Het Nieuwe Bouwen* for its aesthetics combined with social and technical concerns. Expansive glass ribbon windows, steel, and concrete, as epitomized in Zonnestraal, were defining matters of this aesthetic. Moreover, *Het Nieuwe Bouwen* was influenced by the two modern groups that preceded it – *De Stijl* and the Amsterdam School. Both groups

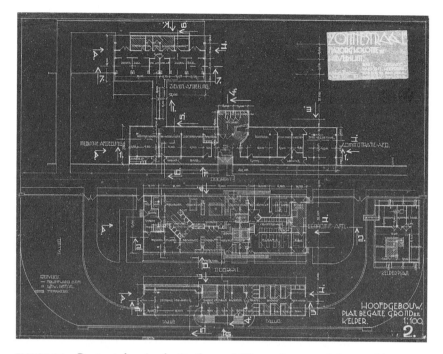

FIGURE 2.6 Contract drawing by Duiker and Bijvoet for ground floor and basement plans of main building.

Het Nieuwe Instituut/DUDO collection, inv. nr.

approached the making of architecture as an artistic process and, as art historian Helen Searing writes, "saw [the] architect as a *bouwkunstenaar*, an inspired creator capable of infusing matter with spirit, rather than as a *bouwmeester*, a master builder concerned chiefly with construction and with fulfilling the practical requirements of the program."[17] At Zonnestraal, the infusion of matter with spirit lies at the core of its transparency.

Ideas behind *Het Nieuwe Bouwen* grew out of two modern architect associations formed in the Netherlands: *Opbouw* and *De 8*, founded in 1920 in Rotterdam and 1927 in Amsterdam, respectively. These groups rejected the old society of the 19th century and envisioned a new utopia. *Opbouw* membership included Mart Stam and Johannes van Loghem, both of whom were communists and supporters of the Russian Revolution.[18] Duiker and his engineer Wiebenga joined *De 8* in 1928. The two organizations would merge in 1932 to form the Dutch voice of functionalists, *Het Nieuwe Bouwen* and jointly start the magazine *De 8 en Opbouw*.[19] In 1928, prominent European architects held the inaugural Congrès Internationaux d'Architecture Modern (CIAM) conference in La Sarraz, Switzerland. The visions of *Nieuwe Bouwen* were closely aligned with those of the CIAM manifesto from La Sarraz. CIAM's aim was to provide an architectural response to the changing world following World War I. The group's founding members were some of the most prominent avant-gardes of the time, including Le Corbusier from Switzerland, and Gerrit Rietveld, Mart Stam, and H. Berlage from the Netherlands.[20] The 1928 CIAM declaration included a call for new materials, construction techniques, and the ideals of light, sun, air, and hygiene.[21] Similarly, *Nieuwe Bouwen* promoted the freeing of structure from unnecessary weight, liberating the structure both materially and spiritually. The Zonnestraal Sanatorium was among the *Nieuwe Bouwen* buildings, which included the Technical School in Groningen (1922) by W.G. Wiebenga and L.C. van der Vlugt, and the Van Nelle Factory in Rotterdam (1926–1930) by J.A. Brinkman and L.C. van der Vlugt.[22] Zonnestraal evokes German architecture critic Adolf Behne's definition of functionalism, which he contrasts to rationalism. Behne stated that, in functional buildings, dimensions and characters of buildings are tailored to each use. This results in specific buildings that may not be easily adaptable and have a short life span, of which Zonnestraal is an example. In contrast, a rationalist building can adapt with relative ease to different uses, as in the case of the Van Nelle Factory in Rotterdam, a coffee, tea, and tobacco factory which has been renovated into a conference center and offices.[23]

Furthermore, Zonnestraal represents a particular pillar in social *verzuiling*, or separation of a society by religious and political beliefs. Dutch society of the early 1900s fell into one of three pillars, or *zuil* in Dutch: Catholic, Protestant, or General, the latter of which included socialists, atheists, and those from other religions, including many Jewish workers. Each pillar had their broadcasting stations, unions, schools, housing corporations, and other organizations. Leaders of the "General" Diamond Workers' Union in Amsterdam created a group that was open to people of all religious and political backgrounds; in other words, to be ideologically transparent.[24] When looking to commission an architect, the union, led by Henri Polak and Jan van Zutpen, approached Berlage. Berlage had previously designed their General Diamond Workers' Union building of 1900 in Amsterdam, a fortress-like masonry building elevated on a pedestal, nicknamed "the Stronghold." Preoccupied with other projects, Berlage recommended two young architects who had impressed him in their winning competition entry for the State Academy of Fine Arts.[25] Duiker and Bijvoet were classmates from secondary school through to the Faculty of Architecture of the Technical High School of Delft, graduating in 1913.[26] They had entered and won a few design competitions and built housing in The Hague, but were relatively unknown at the time of Zonnestraal's commission. In 1919, the Copper Wire End Fund purchased a farmland estate in Hilversum[27] and, in the same year, Duiker and Bijvoet were commissioned for the sanatorium project. Though the initial plans for Zonnestraal were drawn that year, the architects designed a number of small projects for the client – including a laundromat that would collect diamond dust from the workers' overalls – until enough money was raised to finally begin construction in 1927.[28] Before the sanatorium construction began, Bijvoet left for Paris in 1925 to work with Pierre Charreau on Maison de Verre, a legendary work of glass architecture and a risk-taking endeavor for its use of glass blocks by St. Gobain, which were relatively untested for exterior use. Upon Duiker's death at the age of 44 in 1935, Bijvoet returned to complete Duiker's last project, the Gooiland Hotel and Theater Complex.[29]

During the construction of Zonnestraal, the union made frequent mention of the construction work's progress in their weekly publication. However, they

FIGURE 2.7 "Zonnestraaldag" (Zonnestraal Day) were organized to raise funds for the sanatorium. Poster for "Zonnestraalday" September 25, 1926 designed by Jan Duiker.
Institute for Social History, Amsterdam.

FIGURE 2.8 Poster for "Zonnestraaldag" (Zonnestraal Day) September 25, 1929 designed by Albert Hahn, Jr.

Dutch Institute for Sound and Vision.

became silent after the building neared completion, presumably because the design did not match Polak and Zutpen's expectations.[30] For the older generation including Berlage, Polak, and Zutpen, liberation of the working mass meant emulating the bourgeois; they modeled their architecture on castles, palaces, or temples. Consequently, the white, machine-like sanatorium was far removed from the prevailing cultural conventions of thick and opaque masonry buildings. This departure from the norm, through the introduction of new construction materials and techniques, was precisely what Duiker aimed for. "For Duiker's generation the emancipation of the working class went hand-in-hand with a new cultural norm, which took no notice of the prevailing norm," writes Dutch architectural historian Herman van Bergeijk.[31] Despite the client's initial hesitation, the forward appearance of a modern building reflected the ideology of a union that stood for transparency, as well as the function it served, to deliver air and light to the recovering patients (Figures 2.7 and 2.8).

Financial and Spiritual Economy

The glass transparency at Zonnestraal, in which the glass nearly disappears as immaterial, resulted from Duiker's disciplined optimization of materials. He economized construction by finding reciprocal relationships between the short life span of a sanatorium, and the client's programmatic demands and scarce financial resources.[32] Instead of wood which can absorb moisture and trap dirt, he worked with concrete, presumably to meet the hygienic requirements of treating a contagious disease.[33] Partly to save money raised by the union workers, as well as to achieve their aesthetic goals, Duiker and the structural engineer Jan Wiebenga carefully shaved off excess materials until no more could be removed. Wiebenga had returned from working for civil engineering and construction firms in the US, where he had learned about reinforced concrete and balloon framing, both of which facilitated lighter and thinner structures.[34] Wiebenga published an article in the periodical *Gewapend Beton* (1926) about American light-frame construction, in which plaster is applied to a metal lathe attached to studs, a construction detail used for non-load-bearing walls at Zonnestraal.[35] Wiebenga was pragmatic in his choice of material use and dimensions of structural members. He would sometimes propose a heavier structure if it cost less in materials or execution. Duiker's decisions were guided more by spiritual economy, emphasizing optimized use of each material. Each component would be tailored to the acting forces, at the cost of increasing the labor.[36]

Despite the custom-designed components, the building was efficiently and speedily built in adherence with the Dutch concrete construction regulations of the time. The construction was based on a three-meter module within which the architects tailored spaces for each function.[37] The Dutch 1918 Concrete Regulations allowed the formwork of the floors with a span of three meters to be removed after one week of curing, instead of the four weeks for longer span buildings. The shorter curing period enabled the contractors to meet the strict time window of six months. Consequently, the patient rooms in the linear buildings were three-meter cubes, and 1.5-meter cantilevers provided terraces in the south and a corridor in the north. As De Jonge observed, "The building is almost like a functional diagram enclosed by a steel, glass and plaster envelope" (Figure 2.9).[38] Duiker sometimes characterized his concrete buildings as an *"étagère"* enclosed by a glass skin.[39] An *étagère* is a French cabinet with slender posts and open shelves, without doors, for displaying precious objects. The delicacy and openness of Zonnestraal's structure, as well as the fragile state of the recovering tuberculosis patients, make this analogy especially fitting.

With materials reduced to the minimum, the building took on an exceptional delicacy and transparency. Importantly, Duiker's notion of economy was not only monetary – minimizing excess materials wherever possible – but also spiritual. In his view, monetary and spiritual economy were innately tied to each other, such that

FIGURE 2.9 Concrete structure with curtain walls removed during restoration. Duiker often characterized his concrete buildings as an "*étagère*" (French cabinet with slender posts and open shelves) enclosed by a glass skin.

Wessel de Jonge Architecten BNA.

> this spiritual economy leads to the most appropriate construction, depending on the material used and evolves steadily towards dematerialization, spiritu-alization … It is undoubtedly the intrinsic economy of the material that enables us to achieve more and to satisfy higher spiritual demands more truly than our forefathers were able to do.[40]

Duiker appears to associate light, diaphanous structure with spirivalty. His objective for economy of materials aligned not only with dematerialization but also with the short life span of this building. Duiker was cognizant of the building's intended impermanence. He selected concrete and glass that would last just long enough to accommodate the short life expectancy of the sanator-ium. As a result, the curtain walls are appropriately ephemeral. For example, he used galvanized steel window frames, which were prone to deterioration from rusting, and planned for the patients to participate in the building main-tenance. Over the 30 years, the patients painted the steel mullions regularly as a part of occupational therapy.[41]

Duiker had critics on his approach to economy of means. H.P. Berlage criticized him for comprising integrity in attempting to build as quickly and cheaply as possible. He said to Duiker about his work, "inspiration, intuition, architectural capacity, have led you to the furthest technical extreme and at that point spiritual values are missing."[42] To this criticism, Duiker responded,

> But the strongest prime impulse lives in us in every cultural expression, in science and in every natural phenomenon. This inspiration is valuable for it follows the laws of economy. Nature itself demonstrates this cosmic law ... Often financial and spiritual economy go hand-in-hand to make all these achievements possible, but the result we see before us is solely the work of the spirit.[43]

Duiker's aspiration for economy was not only about cost reduction or efficiency but also spiritual, akin to nature's way of optimizing performance. The fragile, impermanent beauty of Zonnestraal's glass is like those of the lightweight, sheer wings of a mayfly with a fleeting life span of just one day to mate and die.

Building Techniques and Hygiene

Zonnestraal was built on the ideal that "a healthy society makes full use of the available modern technology."[44] This approach to well-being through current

FIGURE 2.10 In Dresselhuys Pavilion, patients' beds pulled out from their rooms to take in fresh air and light.

Institute for Social History, Amsterdam (1950–1974).

building technology closely aligned with the architectural ideologies of *Nieuwe Bouwen* and CIAM. Duiker and the structural engineer Wiebenga made Zonnestraal a testing ground for the most current state of building science, often testing industrial construction methods on-site with handmade prototypes.[45] Zonnestraal is one of numerous modern buildings in which architecture was reconfigured according to new scientific findings on diseases. From the late 1800s, medical professionals recommended heliotherapy, or deliberate exposure to sunlight, to counter damp, dark unsanitary housing conditions that were believed to cause tuberculosis.[46] Nineteenth century architecture was demonized for lack of daylight and ventilation, and the attempts to improve living conditions in overcrowded cities coincided with the emergence of modern architecture. Modern architectural features of flat roofs, balconies, and terraces built in steel and concrete were not only a means to a fashionable suntan but also a prevention of, if not a cure for, tuberculosis.

In the patient pavilions, reinforced concrete slabs and columns enabled long span and unobstructed views, and the patient rooms were configured as fingers that reached out to the landscape for exposure to light. The steel frames facilitated horizontal bands of windows that allowed daylight to stream into the buildings. Long, horizontal openings were divided into fixed panes and casement windows to allow cross ventilation through corridors and patient rooms. In the patients' rooms, on the side opposite the hallway, glass doors framed in thin steel members opened directly out onto a balcony, where the patients' beds were pulled out into the open daylight, allowing them to take in fresh air (Figures 2.10 and 2.11). The differentiation of the outer walls was another novel construction approach that enabled freely open façades. By differentiating the load-bearing columns from the non-load-bearing infills, façades could have larger openings, allowing light and air to flow freely.[47] Whereas Semper and Berlage placed significance on the joint, Duiker minimized the joint for hygienic and economic purposes.[48] In accordance with his belief in spiritual economy, Duiker optimized each material; concrete beams were tapered and girders were haunched, their profiles closely following the structural load diagram (Figures 2.12 and 2.13).[49]

In this machine for light and air, many tuberculosis patients recovered and gained occupational skills to go back to their communities; the building participated in the making of a healthy, modern society.[50] The newspaper *Het Centrum* likened the buildings of Zonnestraal to an ocean liner in which every square inch was used.[51] Furthermore, like a ship in the sea, the sanatorium was also removed from the daily lives of the factory workers, isolated out in nature (Figure 2.14). Such analogies delighted Duiker. These qualities were consistent with Le Corbusier's principals of modern architecture as set out in *Vers une architecture* of 1931.[52] The building had a hygienic aura – it was a machine for healing.[53]

FIGURE 2.11 Steel-framed glass doors of Dresselhuys Pavilion pivoted directly out onto a balcony, where the patients' beds were pulled out for exposure to open daylight and fresh air.

Photograph: Author (2018).

Glazing

Although glass has ancient roots, changes in production methods have expanded available glass building products. Relatively new as a building material, glass was, due to cost and fragility, used sparingly until the Industrial Revolution, when it became an indisputable material of that period. Glass in early modern buildings saw a significant shift in material properties and in the resulting effects. Duiker and Bijvoet detailed Zonnestraal's glass curtain wall to minimize obstructive mullions. Interior paint colors augmented the transparent reading of the ribbon windows. The light blue mullion lines framed the views of the forest against the whitewashed walls, causing the windows to seemingly disappear into the sky. To complement the light blue window frames, the lower parts of the walls were finished with a light pastel yellow mineral paint,

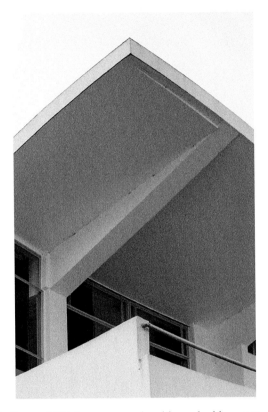

FIGURE 2.12   Duiker and Wiebenga tapered and haunched beams to shave off excess concrete material.

Photograph: Author (2018).

pulling the colors of the sun into the interior (Figure 2.15). The ceilings and upper parts of the walls were whitewashed over a lime plaster finish. Wessel de Jonge, one of the architects who during Zonnestraals' restoration removed the thick, green, aluminum frames and replaced them with thin steel frames painted light blue, writes, "The heavenly blue shade of the casing, with a remarkable touch of violet, makes the steel frames dissolve against the sky."[54] Even building corners became glass curtain walls, with load-bearing concrete columns set back from the perimeter walls. The material properties and assembly details of glass, combined with those of concrete and steel, contribute to the defining character of glass transparency at Zonnestraal.

Prior to the middle of the 19th century, window frames were built predominantly out of wood. Joseph Paxton's Crystal Palace of 1851 made a radical mark by using cast iron for the structure to reduce maintenance costs and to

FIGURE 2.13 Common room in Dresselhuys Pavilion shows exposed haunched concrete beams. Expansive windows bring in panoramic view of the forest and fresh air.

Photograph: Author (2018).

FIGURE 2.14 Zonnestraal Sanatorium was likened to a ship in the sea (1929).

Institute for Social History, Amsterdam.

FIGURE 2.15 Window frames of the main building are painted light blue to merge with the sky, and walls in light pastel yellow to pull in the colors of the sun to the interior.

Photograph: Author (2018).

proof against the weather, although Paxton incorporated wood throughout for beams and gutters. Steel window manufacturers began to form around this time and challenged the dominance of timber windows. When World War I broke out, steel window manufactures directed their efforts towards munition production, from which they learned techniques that they later applied to window manufacturing.[55] Steel frame windows from the British manufacturer Crittall were installed, including in the corners of buildings at the Bauhaus (1926) by Walter Gropius and at the Finsbury Health Center (1936) by Berthold Lubetkin and Tecton.[56]

Zonnestraal was built in the midst of a brief boom in curtain wall technology in the second half of the 1920s. The sanatorium broke ground during the surge in construction industry that would be halted by the Great Depression of the 1930s until the end of World War II.[57] In 1928, Duiker and Bijvoet experimented with a cutting-edge prototypical curtain wall in the main building. The window frames of the main building had a steel profile thickness of only 25 mm. They were pre-assembled in a workshop and mounted on-site against steel posts that spanned between the floors. To minimize material, each window module came with a vertical steel jamb only on one side, with the other side supported by the adjacent window unit. As a result, a single, long continuous window appeared to span the entire 108 feet of the building length. In fact, the lack of dimensional tolerance in both the steel frames and in installation caused the glass to break easily. The frames were also too thin and unstable to support a casement window on top, so the large casement window was divided into three smaller ones to prevent warping and breaking. The architects learned from the prototype of the main building, and in the third building that followed in 1931 they specified a 32/37 mm profile frame, with smaller, side-hung casement windows.[58] Smaller windows meant more frequent spacing of steel, which resulted not only in higher material costs but also more visual obstructions. Duiker's spiritual economy was dependent on the most efficient use of materials, which resulted in greater lightness and transparency of the glass walls.

In addition to the curtain wall technology, the glass sheets themselves are products of a short period spanning between the times of blown glass and machine-made float glass. Zonnestraal predated Alastair Pilkington's 1952 invention of float glass, a process by which a thin layer of molten glass is poured on top of molten tin. This invention enabled production of sheet glass with a greater smoothness, flatness, and accuracy than the preceding drawn glass, or the blown and flattened cylinder glass. Pilkington's mass-manufactured float glass led to its commercialization. In contrast, the windows of Zonnestraal were single-lite drawn glass. Invented by Émile Fourcault of Belgium, drawn glass is made by drawing – or pulling – molten glass in a linear pit upward against gravity, to form a flat sheet. At Zonnestraal, the fragile thinness of the drawn glass sheet is underscored by the delicacy of the steel frame that maximizes the building's transparency. In comparison to today's typically strengthened, coated, and insulated glass, Zonnestraal's windows appear delicate, colorless, and crystal clear, possessing traces of the production process in the visible ripple patterns. In congruence with the original vision of the light concrete building, delicate glass membranes are supported by steel frames that appear impossibly thin by today's standards. Duiker and Bijvoet made optical qualities of glass clear and steel frames light; in fact, their light- and heat-transmission rates were so high that such curtain walls would be prohibited by today's energy code. This was, however, hardly relevant for a building intended for curing the patients in open air.

Obsolescence of Function

By the mid-1950s, the invention of drug therapy rendered sanatoria obsolete. Zonnestraal was converted to a general hospital in 1957.[59] The open balconies of the first residential pavilion became fully enclosed between 1955 and 1958, drastically altering its lightness and transparency. Around 1976, the main building went through a radical renovation. The main entrance was moved to the former location of the kosher kitchen, and almost all interior partitions were removed and reconfigured.[60] The slender steel window frames were replaced with wide, aluminum-framed double glazing. In the 1980s the second residential pavilion stood relatively unaltered, but glass had fallen out, either through vandalism or deterioration of the frames and structures that supported the curtain walls (Figure 2.16). Broken windows exposed the concrete and rebars to the elements and caused them to corrode.[61] When the general hospital joined another hospital in town in the early 1990s, the complex was largely vacated. Photographs of Zonnestraal from the 1980s and 90s, with double glazing framed in wide aluminum mullions, show the building robbed of its buoyancy and dignity. The striking disparity between the original and the renovated building further underscores the significance of material and detail choices in the reading of glass transparency. The renovation from this period demonstrates how architectural vision can be violated when materials are updated with little consideration for significance of original materiality.

FIGURE 2.16 Deteriorated Dresselhuys Pavilion in 2000, prior to renovation. In the early 1990s the buildings were largely vacated.

Photograph: Hans Hoogenboom. Streekarchief Gooi en Vechtstreek (early 2000s).

Restoration and Preservation of a Building Designed for Brevity

As seen in Zonnestraal, the contemporary restoration of an early modern building allows a comparative analysis of a restored building against the original. How are changes in glass technology reflected in decisions and ideologies of earlier buildings? In 1994, the Dutch government decided to restore Zonnestraal.[62] The restoration was undertaken by architects Hubert-Jan Henket and Wessel de Jonge, co-founders of Docomomo (Documentation and Conservation of Buildings, Sites and Neighborhoods of the Modern Movement) International.[63] Their work followed extensive research into the original construction at Delft University of Technology. De Jonge reflects that the restoration of Zonnestraal "proved an unprecedented source of knowledge and hands-on experience with early modern building technology and its preservation."[64] The restoration indeed revealed how the readings of Zonnestraal's glass transparency were dependent upon changes in materials and construction details.

During the restoration, De Jonge and Henket faced critical questions regarding the preservation of a modern glass building. Examining their preservation process reveals Zonnestraal's glass as exclusive to a particular place and culture in Dutch history. When the original architects' intent was to amplify transparency, does it violate the design to replace the windows with today's insulated or laminated float glass, in order to meet thermal efficiency for current standards? Furthermore, how should qualities of glass at the time of construction in the 1920s be preserved during restoration? In maintaining the original qualities of glass, the specification of glass is critical.[65] The architects carefully assessed whether to follow as closely as possible the original specification of single-lite glass, or to replace with present-day insulated glass panels. As a result, the glass used in the restoration is not the same everywhere as it was in the original building (Figure 2.17). In consultation with building physics consultants DGMR, the architects decided to install single glazing in areas that did not require careful climate control, primarily the hallways and the main hall upstairs, where there are no occupants immediately adjacent to the curtain walls.[66]

The details and physical properties of glass radically alter a building's transparency. De Jonge notes that the Zonnestraal would read completely different had the glazing been replaced with all insulated units with today's standard float glass.[67] Drawn glass like that from 1928 was made using sand with a lower iron content, which resulted in purer, colorless glass. In contrast, today's standard glass has a greenish tint from iron oxide, which is added to accelerate melting rate in the manufacturing stage.[68] In addition to the color, today's less flawed, machine-made float glass would have eliminated the vertical ripples of the original building. For the restoration, low-iron drawn glass was imported from Lithuania to stay true to the original color and patterns from the 1920s. The cross-axial layout of the main building creates places, such as the entrance vestibule, where one looks

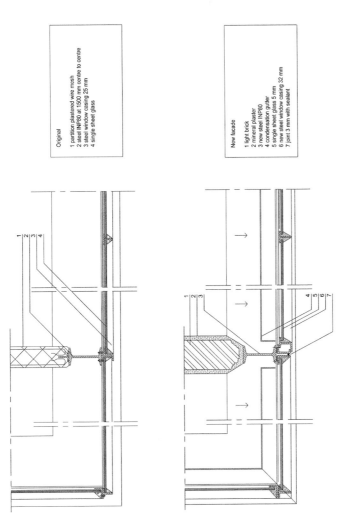

Original

1 partition plastered wire mesh
2 steel INP80 at 1500 mm centre to centre
3 steel window casing 25 mm
4 single sheet glass

New facade

1 light brick
2 mineral plaster
3 new steel INP80
4 condensation gutter
5 single sheet glass 5 mm
6 new steel window casing 32 mm
7 joint 3 mm with sealant

FIGURE 2.17 Top: plan details of a corner of original 1928 single-lite glass. Bottom: plan detail of the same corner in 2001 renovation, in which the corner is turned with two sheets of low-iron, single-lite drawn glass. The adjacent panel to the right is an insulated glass unit with low-iron drawn glass for outside light only.

Wessel de Jonge Architecten BNA (2001).

through four layers of glass as a time (Figure 2.18). In these locations, the attention to glass color was particularly important,[69] as the tint becomes amplified with multiple layers of glass.

In such space as the offices, where single glazing is insufficient for today's thermal comfort, the architects specified a custom assembly: an 11 mm thick double-glazing unit fabricated in a Belgian factory, with a gray uPVC spacer made in Italy. Where the single and double glazing are adjacent to each other, the windows have the Lithuanian low-iron, drawn glass on the outside to maintain consistent appearance.[70] To keep the cost down, instead of using the custom glass on both the inside and the outside, the inner pane is a single layer, low-iron *Starphire* Ultra-Clear™ float glass – a readily available product manufactured in the US by Pittsburg Plate Glass (PPG).[71]

FIGURE 2.18 A view through multiple sheets of glass at a corner in the main building, where clear, colorless glass is particularly important.

Photograph: Author (2018).

FIGURE 2.19 Dresselhuys Pavilion's window-lined corridor with patient rooms along the right-hand side. During the renovation, these windows were replaced with insulated glass, allowing more possible functions of the building in the future.

Photograph: Author (2018).

When Zonnestraal was designed, healthcare standards advocated keeping windows open at all times, including the winter; it was the opposite of a tightly sealed building. Energy efficiency upgrades to meet today's standards are impossible without losing the essential architectural character of Zonnestraal.[72] In the Dresselhuys Pavilion (the second residential pavilion), all the patient rooms received the double-glazed units used in the main building (Figure 2.19). The reason was twofold. This building has rows of private patient rooms arranged so that one does not look through multiple layers of glass walls as in the main building. Second, the building did not have an occupant type specified at the time of restoration. To allow many possible uses in the future, therefore, the Pavilion was restored with insulated glass walls.[73]

Time-Specific Glass Transparency

Zonnestraal's glass transparency was shaped by a complex set of ideals and construction technologies specific to its time, place, and program. The glass appears to eradicate barriers between the sunlight and the interior, symbolizing equality for the union workers and conquering tuberculosis through architecture. In accordance with the ideals of *Nieuwe Bouwen*, Duiker and Bijvoet spiritually freed the structure from excess weight by experimenting with the newest construction techniques, structures, and materials. Only in this narrow time period between the wars in the Netherlands, for a programmatic function with a brief life span, would such a delicate building be sensible. There is a fragile beauty to Duiker's Zonnestraal, as Peter Smithson described in 1962:

> His buildings are just buildings, and when one says that their poetry is slightly mad, it is I think because they have a purity and faith that we find almost too hard to bear, it shines out of the smallest detail, the windows for example at Sonnestraal, and the small white walls round the trees.[74]

Both the expansive, dematerialized windows and the low, white walls transition the building to the landscape, connecting the bedrooms to the trees in the forest.

Henket and De Jonge's restoration of the glass walls further underscores the differences between the glass transparencies of single-lite drawn glass of the 1920s and contemporary insulated glass units with float glass, the standard of new glass buildings today; the former appears colorless and nearly nonexistent in contrast to today's coated, tinted, and insulated glass. The available glass technology, means for construction, and expectations for thermal comfort are a few architectural factors that evolve over time and, subsequently, engender culture- and time-specific glass transparency. The creation of an experimental period between the wars, Zonnestraal's glass is rendered nearly immaterial through Duiker's objective to economize while healing patients through exposure to light and air. This building serves to comprehend the changing reading of glass over the next eight decades. The following chapters uncover different types of glass transparencies that are shaped by a variety of circumstances.

Notes

1   Bruno Reichlin, "The Original Splendour Regained," in Paul Meurs and Marie-Thérèse van Thoor, Eds., *Sanatorium Zonnestraal: The History and Restoration of a Modern Monument* (Rotterdam: nai010, 2011), 239.
2   Paul Overy, *Light, Air & Openness: Modern Architecture between the Wars* (London: Thames & Hudson, 2007), 19.
3   John F. Murray, Dean E. Schraufnagel, and Philip C. Hopewell, "Treatment of Tuberculosis. A Historical Perspective," *Annals of the American Thoracic Society* 12, no. 12 (December 2015), 1749–1759.

4 Murray et al., "Treatment of Tuberculosis."

5 Margaret Campbell, "What Tuberculosis Did for Modernism," *Medical History* 49, no. 4 (2005), 464–470.

6 Campbell, "What Tuberculosis Did for Modernism," 467. In 1930, Alvar Aalto visited Zonnestraal, which impressed him and influenced his design of Paimio.

7 Overy, *Light, Air & Openness*, 22.

8 Overy, *Light, Air & Openness*, 14.

9 Wessel de Jonge and Paul Meurs, "The Zonnestraal Aftercare Colony: Design and Buildings," in Meurs and van Thoor, Eds., *Sanatorium Zonnestraal*, 77.

10 Overy, *Light, Air & Openness*, 15.

11 Paul Scheerbart and Bruno Taut, *Glass Architecture, by Paul Scheerbart; and Alpine Architecture, by Bruno Taut*. Ed. Dennis Sharp (New York: Praeger, 1972).

12 Hans Maria Wingler, *The Bauhaus: Weimar, Dessau, Berlin, Chicago*, trans. Wolfgang Jabs and Basil Gilbert (Cambridge, MA: MIT Press, 1969), 31.

13 Rosemarie Haag Bletter, "Interpretation of Glass Dreams: Expressionist Architecture and the History of the Crystal Metaphor," *Journal of the Society of Architectural Historians* 40, no. 1 (March, 1981), 37–38.

14 Wessel de Jonge, "'Zonnestraal': Restoration of a Transitory Architecture: Concept, Planning and Realisation in the Context of Authenticity," (Paper presented at Seventh International DOCOMOMO Technology Seminar, Vyborg September - 18–19, 2003), 4.

15 Erik Mattie, *Functionalism in the Netherlands* (Amsterdam: Architecture & Naturas, 1995), 5–27.

16 Helen Searing, "The Dutch Scene: Black and White and Red All over," *Art Journal* 43, no. 2 (Summer, 1983), 170.

17 Searing, "The Dutch Scene," 172.

18 Searing, "The Dutch Scene," 170.

19 Ben Rebel, "The Appearance and Disappearance of the Term *Nieuwe Zakelijkheid* in Dutch Modern Architecture," in Ralf Grüttemeier, Klaus Beekman, and Ben Rebel, Eds., *Neue Sachlichkeit and Avant-Garde* (Amsterdam: Rodopi, 2013), 140.

20 Mattie, *Functionalism in the Netherlands*, 13.

21 Mattie, *Functionalism in the Netherlands*, 13.

22 Reyer Kras et al., *Het Nieuwe Bouwen, Amsterdam 1920–1960* (Delft: Delft University Press; Stedelijk Museum, 1983), 8–10.

23 Hubert-Jan Henket and Wessel de Jonge, "A Restoration Concept for Modern Movement Architecture," in Meurs and van Thoor, Eds., *Sanatorium Zonnestraal*, 99.

24 Wessel de Jonge, restoration architect for Zonnestraal, interview by author, Rotterdam, March 14, 2019.

25 Jan Molema, "The Zonnestraal Commission," in Meurs and van Thoor, Eds., *Sanatorium Zonnestraal*, 62–65.

26 Robert Vickery, "Bijvoet and Duiker," *Perspecta* 13/14 (1971), 133–134.

27 Annette Koenders, "Centuries-Old Landscape: History of the Design of the Zonnestraal Estate," in Meurs and van Thoor, Eds., *Sanatorium Zonnestraal*, 67.

28 Molema, "The Zonnestraal Commission," 62–64.

29 Vickery, "Bijvoet and Duiker," 130–160.

30 Herman van Bergeijk, "Architecture and 'Spiritual' Economy," in Meurs and van Thoor, Eds., *Sanatorium Zonnestraal*, 75.

31 van Bergeijk, "Architecture and 'Spiritual' Economy," 75.

32 De Jonge, "Zonnestraal," 4.

33 De Jonge, "Zonnestraal," 3.

34 De Jonge, interview, 2019.

35 Wessel de Jonge, "Nieuwe Bouwen in Practice," in Meurs and van Thoor, Eds., *Sanatorium Zonnestraal*, 116.

36 De Jonge, "Nieuwe Bouwen in Practice," 112.
37 De Jonge, "Zonnestraal," 3.
38 De Jonge, "Zonnestraal," 3.
39 Wessel de Jonge, email message to author, July 24, 2019.
40 Jan Duiker, "Berlage en de 'NieuweZakelijkheid'," *De 8 en Opbouw* 1932, 1, 43–51, cited in Aimee de Back, Sabine Berndsen and Camiel Berns, Eds., *Een zeer aangenaam verblijf: het dienstbodenhuis van J Duiker op sanatorium Zonnestraal. A space of their own: the servants' house by J Duiker at Zonnestraal sanatorium* (Rotterdam: 010 Publishers, 1996), 15.
41 De Jonge, "Zonnestraal," 4.
42 Vickery, "Bijvoet and Duiker," 156.
43 *Architectural Forum*, 1 (1962), quoted in Robert Vickery, "Bijvoet and Duiker," 156–157. The original source cited did not contain the attributed quotation.
44 van Bergeijk, "Architecture and 'Spiritual' Economy," 73.
45 De Jonge, "Zonnestraal," 4.
46 Campbell, "What Tuberculosis Did for Modernism," 464–467.
47 De Jonge, "Nieuwe Bouwen in Practice," 117.
48 van Bergeijk, "Architecture and 'Spiritual' Economy," 73.
49 De Jonge, "Nieuwe Bouwen in Practice," 110.
50 van Bergeijk. "Architecture and 'Spiritual' Economy," 77.
51 van Bergeijk, "Architecture and 'Spiritual' Economy," 74.
52 Le Corbusier, *Towards a New Architecture*, trans. Frederick Etchells (London: J. Rodker, 1931). Reprint New York: Dover, 1985.
53 van Bergeijk, "Architecture and 'Spiritual' Economy," 74.
54 De Jonge, "Zonnestraal," 9.
55 David Blake, "Windows, Critall and the Modern Movement," in Hubert Henket and Wessel de Jonge, Eds., *Proceedings of the First International DOCOMOMO Conference, Sept. 12–15, 1990* (Eindhoven: DOCOMOMO, 1990), 76.
56 Blake, "Windows, Critall and the Modern Movement," 77.
57 De Jonge, "Zonnestraal," 5.
58 De Jonge, "Zonnestraal," 5.
59 De Jonge, "Zonnestraal," 5.
60 De Jonge, "Zonnestraal," 5.
61 De Jonge, "Zonnestraal," 6.
62 Fons Asselbergs, "Quality Hurts: Government and Government Agency Policy," in Meurs and van Thoor, Eds., *Sanatorium Zonnestraal*, 146. In 1994, the Dutch Ministry of Welfare, Health and Cultural Affairs pledged a subsidy of 7.5 million guilders for Zonnestraal's restoration.
63 Docomomo is "a non-profit organization dedicated to the documentation and conservation of buildings, sites and neighborhoods of the modern movement." Henket is now a retired professor and De Jonge a current professor, both in Heritage and Design at the Technical University of Delft.
64 De Jonge, "Zonnestraal," 1.
65 Wessel de Jonge and Hubert-Jan Henket, "The Restoration," in Meurs and van Thoor, Eds., *Sanatorium Zonnestraal*, 191.
66 De Jonge and Henket, "The Restoration," 191.
67 De Jonge and Henket, "The Restoration," 191.
68 R.L. Shute and A.E. Badger, "Effect of Iron Oxide on Melting of Glass," *Journal of the American Ceramic Society* 25 (August 1, 1942), 355, https://ceramics-onlineli brary-wiley-com.ezproxy.lib.vt.edu/doi/abs/10.1111/j.1151-2916.1942.tb14318.x.
69 De Jonge and Henket, "The Restoration," 191.
70 De Jonge, "Zonnestraal," 8–9.

71 De Jonge, "Zonnestraal," 9. PPG is now Vitro Architectural Glass.
72 De Jonge, "Zonnestraal," 6.
73 De Jonge and Henket, "The Restoration," 196.
74 Alison Smithson and Peter Smithson, *The Heroic Period of Modern Architecture* (New York: Rizzoli, 1981), 42.

3

MIRRORING IPSWICH
Contextual Glass Transparency of the Willis Building

Shaped like a grand piano, the curved, three-story Willis Faber and Dumas Headquarters (1975) by Foster Associates[1] in Ipswich, UK is draped from the roof to the sidewalk in dark gray, frameless glass curtain wall in a continuous ribbon (Figure 3.1). In Louis Sullivan's tripartite grammar of a high-rise (base, shaft, and capital), it appears to be nearly all shaft, with deemphasized base and capital. The Willis Building – as it is now called – made pioneering contributions to glass transparency. Notably, the building achieved a breakthrough in the curtain wall system; Foster's team worked with glass manufacturer Pilkington to suspend glass panels from concrete floors by metal corner patch plates, absent of mullions. They realized the dream of frameless glass curtain walls depicted in Mies van der Rohe's drawings of the Freidrichstrasse Skyscraper (1921) and the Glass Skyscraper (1922).

Additionally, the Willis Building presented an alternative approach to an urban glass building that is contextual while radically contrasting the masonry buildings that surround it. In comparison to the freestanding mirrored glass box buildings in the sprawling office parks of the 1960s, or the conventional rectilinear high-rise, Foster's building responds purposely to its urban context. The building fills the boundaries of the irregularly curved medieval streets "like a pancake in a pan,"[2] in Foster's words. The building exhibits mutable readings on and through the glass at different times of the day. In the daytime, the frameless glass curtain wall becomes a scrim on which the masonry buildings across the street appear reflected in the black tinted glass. It denies views into the office, except on occasions where the interior is lit more brightly than the exterior. At night, the building reverses the black piano-like reading: the transparent glass walls expose the illuminated interior and concrete structures like an X-ray (Figure 3.2). While modern and high-tech in appearance, its

FIGURE 3.1 The northwest façade on Princes Street reflects both itself and the building across the street. The main entrance with three revolving doors is located on thr lower left side.

Photograph: Author (2019).

FIGURE 3.2 At night, the transparent glass walls expose the illuminated interior and concrete structures like an X-ray.

Courtesy of Norman Foster Foundation (1971–1975).

undulating footprint and building height echo the city's history. Finally, the building introduces a new kind of idealism through social transparency in the workplace; it realizes latent ideas of Climatroffice, a novel workplace imagined and drawn by Foster and Buckminster Fuller a few years earlier in 1971. The Willis Building cultivated non-hierarchical interactions among employees and employers through architectural elements, such as sky-lit escalators that run visibly through the center of office floors, a pool adjacent to the reception area for employees and their families, and a planted rooftop with a restaurant for meals and breaks.

Building in an English Medieval City

The building was commissioned by the insurance company founded by Henry Willis in 1828 in London. A global leader in the industry, the company insured the ill-fated Titanic in 1912 and in 1972 the moon buggy, the rover vehicle of the NASA Apollo program.[3] At the time of the building commission in 1970, Willis, Faber & Dumas, as the company was called, had a series of buildings throughout London. In 1971, they had 21,000 employees, and the new building would bring 1,200 under one roof. They chose the city of Ipswich for a variety of reasons: its proximity to London, which is an hour by train; good schools; a variety of housing options; closeness to the countryside; and the building's location in an historic city center.[4] The Ipswich city planners were keen to support commercial developments that would bring the prestigious company and employment opportunities. Consequently, they approved a strikingly contemporary architecture proposal that more conservative officials might have denied.[5]

The building occupies the footprints of former buildings that were demolished, while stopping short of the historic Unitarian Meeting House (1700) to its immediate east. "It should preserve and reinforce the street pattern, rather than impose an alien geometry on the site," said Foster at a preliminary presentation to the client in 1971.[6] The seemingly amorphous shape of the building results from tracing the existing streets: the winding medieval streets of Prince and Friars Streets to the north; Franciscan Way to the southwest, which in the 1960s had become a ring road with a roundabout adjacent to the western tip; and another portion of Franciscan Way to the south. The road running on a north–south axis between its east wall and the Unitarian Meeting House defines the only straight portion – and the least visible – of the façade (Figure 3.3).[7] Despite its strikingly contemporary appearance, the history of Ipswich pushed and pulled the perimeter outline of the building.

Initially, some residents of Ipswich reacted adversely. They were skeptical of the virtually black, irregularly shaped glass building that they could not see into during the day. When the interior became visible at night, the office floors were empty with no one working inside, which further intensified the

FIGURE 3.3 Site plans showing existing condition (upper left), final scheme (lower right), and two preliminary schemes. The seemingly amorphous shape of the building results from tracing the existing streets.

Courtesy of Norman Foster Foundation (1971–1975).

mystery of the foreign building.[8] However, the people of Ipswich were given tours of the office and, over time, softened their opinions. In 1991, the Willis Building was listed as a Grade I building by the British government for its architectural significance, becoming the youngest building in England to receive such status and given protection against demolition or alteration.[9]

Contextual Glass

In addition to implementing a radically new frameless curtain wall, the Willis Building introduced a novel way for a high-tech glass building to be contextual. The building was shaped by context in ways that defy conventional historic references. The faceted glass panels result in fractured reflections of the surrounding cityscape; the buildings across the streets, ranging from Gothic to Brutalist, are presented as distorted reflections continuously recomposed as the viewers walk along the building (Figure 3.4). The building's instrumentality operates much like the concave mirrors one finds at street corners, alerting pedestrians of the cars and busses approaching around the corner. The dark,

FIGURE 3.4 The faceted glass panels depict the surrounding buildings as an assembly of fractured reflections.

Courtesy of Norman Foster Foundation (1971–1975).

transparent glass of the Willis Building reflects back to the city the street that shaped it; the glass panels depict the surrounding buildings like clusters of partially assembled jigsaw puzzles.

The ways in which the Willis Building's façade confounds the viewers are similar to those observed in the works by Light and Space artists of the 1960s, including James Turrell, Robert Irwin, and Dan Graham. In their work, materials' edges and joints are detailed to dissolve. In Turrell's *Skyspace* installations, the edges of the ceiling aperture that frame the sky are tapered so that the edges appear as thin as a sheet of paper. In Irwin's gossamer scrim walls, the material edges appear to dissolve with light, blurring the boundaries between material and space. Dan Graham's pavilions often comprise steel frames, mirrors, and glass with reflective coating. As viewers move around the space, they voyeuristically see themselves seeing, while watching others do the same. Viewers' perception of the real versus the virtual images becomes blurred in Graham's constructs. Similar to these artists' work, at the Willis Building the boundaries between reflected sky and the actual sky become blurred, particularly seamlessly at twilight when the glass appears to merge with the sky (Figure 3.5). This blurring is underscored by reflections of itself mirrored, along with buildings across the street, on the building's façade; the Willis

FIGURE 3.5   At twilight, the glass appears to merge with the sky.

Photograph: Author (2019).

Building not only simply mirrors but also dissolves and reassembles itself and the surrounding landscape.

Boston's John Hancock Tower, designed by Henry Cobb of I. M. Pei and Partners and completed one year later than the Willis Building in 1976, offers a comparison to the Willis Building. Its form was shaped by its location on Copley Square and its adjacency to H.H. Richardson's Trinity Church. It takes, on the one hand, a dissimilar approach to context by erecting a 62-floor "notched rhomboid" glass tower in a rectangular site and, on the other, a similar approach to the Willis Building in being both silent and assertive. Cobb refers to the stance of the Hancock Tower as a form of poetry and silence:

> The building's restraint to the point of muteness, its refusal to reveal any-thing other than its obsession with its urban context, is surely its greatest strength but also its ultimate limitation as a work of architecture. Despite the forcefulness of its gesture, the tower remains virtually speechless, and this resolute self-denial is, in the end, both its triumph and its tragedy.[10]

Public opposition towards the Willis Building was mild compared to the shock and horror that the Hancock Tower elicited. However, the Willis Building, in some ways, shares the muteness of the Hancock Tower. The reflective, dark gray façade that reveals very little of the interior office appears forbidding. Its front doors located on the side opposite the face with the highest traffic, make the main entrance difficult for visitors to locate. With no entrance canopy, setback, or a change in material to signify an invitation, the revolving glass doors are mute (Figure 3.6). Furthermore, despite the dynamic reflections of the neighboring buildings activating the façade, the glass panels are sealed tightly with silicone, with no operable windows or balconies indicating human scale. The building is restrained, and does not reveal employee interactions or expressions in the ways of, for instance, Herman Hertzberger's Centraal Beheer.

Nonetheless, the Willis Building has been celebrated for its novel correlation to the existing townscape. Reyner Banham, in his 1977 essay "Grass above, Glass around," champions the Willis Building for attaining contextualism of the Townscape movement advocated by Gordon Cullen, an influential British urban designer. Cullen authored *Townscape* (1961), a book characterized by his picturesque perspective sketches, primarily of vernacular buildings from the

FIGURE 3.6 With no entrance canopy, setback, or a change in material to signify an invitation, the three revolving glass doors on the northwest façade facing Princes Street appear mute.

Photograph: Author (2019).

winding streets, ports, and town squares of medieval English cities. He wrote, "bring buildings together and collectively they can give visual pleasure which one cannot give separately."[11] Banham contends that the Willis Building, with unapologetically modern language and materials, engenders the picturesque qualities that Cullen advocated. Banham writes the Willis Building possesses "exactly the kinds of visual effects – surprises, truncation, concealment, confrontation – for which *Townscape* always campaigned,"[12] but using an architectural language of high-tech glass that contrasts the brick piazzas, stone arcades, and bell towers in *Townscape*.

Building Organization and a New Concept for Workplaces

The glass transparency of the Willis Building is further shaped by the spatial organization of programs and structure. Foster describes the organization as

FIGURE 3.7 Escalators ascend through the sky-lit central atrium from the lobby to the roof, serving as a place of informal encounters.

Photograph: Author (2019).

a "hamburger" – two office floors sandwiched between the ground floor and the restaurant on the roof.[13] A vertical circulation space with a bank of escalators penetrates through all floors, illuminated by daylight through the glass enclosure of the rooftop restaurant (Figure 3.7). The exposed, white space frame of the roof, visible from all four floors through the atrium, reflects the incoming daylight to brighten the interior. This structure, which enables the flexible arrangement of a single universal space below, would become a key expressive element in Foster's Sainsbury Centre for Visual Arts (1978). Foster credits the Bradbury Building (1893) in Los Angeles, designed by Sumner Hunt, as a precedent for an office building centered around an atrium.[14] The sky-lit atrium of the Bradbury Building (Figure 3.8) houses the elevator, walkways, and stairs in ornate ironwork. The luminosity of the interior atrium presents a striking contrast to the heavy masonry walls on the exterior. The Willis Building's atrium similarly functions as a circulation core and a place of

FIGURE 3.8 The Bradbury Building (1893) in downtown Los Angeles influenced Foster's design of the Willis Building circulation atrium. Oblique view of the central court from the balcony (1960).

Historic American Building Survey; Library of Congress.

informal encounters for employees and, in daylight, emanates luminosity that contrasts the solidity of the dark gray glass seen from the street.

The black glass exterior with curved corners – built with flat, faceted glass panels – calls to mind an Art Deco building from Foster's hometown of Manchester. Foster here credits the curved black glass of the Daily Express Building (1939) for inspiration.[15] The Daily Express Building (Figure 3.9) is clad in pigmented structural glass, a high strength annealed glass developed in 1900 by the Marrietta Manufacturing Company of Indiana as a substitute for natural stone. It was used widely in streamlined Art Deco buildings around the world. On the ground level, the Daily Express Building showcases the printing press situated next to the glass wall. Likewise, Foster exhibits the mechanical equipment (Figure 3.10) located at street level on the west and southwest façades,

FIGURE 3.9 Foster credits the Daily Express Building (1939) by Sir Owen Williams, in his hometown of Manchester, UK, as an influence. The printing press is made visible through a street-level glass curtain wall.

Photograph: John Maltby/RIBA Collections.

FIGURE 3.10 Mechanical equipment of the Willis Building exhibited through glass at street level.

Photograph: View Pictures, Universal Images Group collection (2012).

facing the active traffic roundabout. The machines are curated along the street, made visible to drivers, pedestrians, and bus passengers. The machines creating the movement of air inside are set adjacent to the machines creating the movement of people outside. Unlike Le Corbusier's interest in making modern buildings have the appearance of automobiles or ocean liners, Foster's project connects their performance. At dusk, as the interior becomes brighter than the exterior, the organs of the building become visually exposed through the skin's mutable transparency.

The Willis Building has a 14-meter-square structural grid, with perimeter columns seven meters apart – "a necklace" in Foster's words (Figure 3.11). Floors and columns are cast-in-place concrete. Reinforced concrete waffle floors 750 mm deep, cantilever 1.5 meters beyond the "necklace" of columns, tapering to a thin profile at the exterior edge where they meet the glass (Figure 3.12). Likewise, at the central atrium, the concrete floors also taper. The perimeter zone between the row of columns and the frameless glass walls functions as circulation and is kept free of workstations and furniture. Whereas the ceilings above the desks have mirror-finish aluminum slats, the cantilevered

FIGURE 3.11 Ground floor plan showing "necklace" of columns along the perimeter. Courtesy of Norman Foster Foundation (1971–1975).

zone ceiling is exposed, with its tapered concrete ceiling painted white. By removing the barriers and visual distractions in both the floor and the ceiling, the building's sense of transparency and lightness are amplified for those who work inside, as well as for those who look in at night (Figure 3.13). The building creates a play between the horizontality and verticality: the exterior appearance decidedly emphasizes the horizontality of floor slabs, while the interior underscores the verticality of the central escalator bay and the ascending movement towards the sky.

To allow for future subletting, the floors are subdivided into four sections, each with its own core and fire stairs.[16] Sprinklers enabled all floors to open to the atrium. With no firewalls separating the sections, the building was truly an open floor plan that maximized transparency and eliminated visible barriers in the workplace.[17] Over forty years after the building opened, the Willis Building continues to embrace and benefit from its non-hierarchical, open floor plan. No one has had a private cubical since the building opened. Currently, in 2019, the company seats employees using an "agile desk distribution system." Employees in particular sections of the floor are temporarily designated desks in proximity to other project team members, then redistributed when project members change.[18] In order to prevent obstruction of sight lines

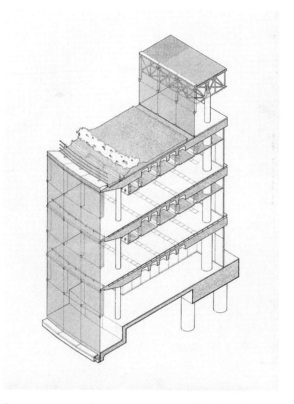

FIGURE 3.12 Cutaway section showing concrete waffle slabs that are tapered at the building perimeter. The ground floor steps down in the perimeter zone to maximize the glass wall coming down to the street.

Courtesy of Norman Foster Foundation (1971–1975).

across floors, filing cabinets are kept below desk height, while taller cabinets are lined against the core walls.

The Dream of Frameless Curtain Walls

Fifty years before the Willis Building's completion, Mies van der Rohe envisioned a skyscraper with frameless glass curtain walls for the Friedrich-strasse Skyscraper competition (1921–1922). The design closely followed the German Revolution of 1918, in which the Kaiser-ruled aristocratic state was replaced by the democratic parliamentary Weiner Republic. Mies wrote that, during such a revolutionary time, new problems must be solved with new forms and materials, rather than with traditional ones.[19] His approach to glass profoundly broke from the past, impressing an historic mark for

FIGURE 3.13 The building's sense of transparency and lightness are amplified for those who work inside, as well as for those who look in at night.

Photograph: English Heritage/Heritage Images/Getty Images (2000).

glass architecture. He wrote that glass buildings depend upon interplay of reflected light, in comparison to the masonry buildings' effects of light and shade.[20] Rejecting traditional masonry walls entirely, his rendering (Figure 3.14) shows a high-rise with façades draped in frameless glass panels against the silhouettes of thin floor slabs. The sharp, faceted façades reach towards the sky, emphasizing the verticality and contrasting the horizontality of surrounding masonry buildings that hug the streets. This divergence from the context is not only in geometry but also in qualities of light and materials; the transparent glass high-rise stands in mutable luminescence like a large crystal with delicate shadows, against the low-rise buildings rendered in dark shadows. This historically significant competition entry was soon followed by the Glass Skyscraper (1922) proposal drawings (Figure 3.15) with their irregularly shaped, amoeba-like plan, suggestive of the Willis Building's implied curves.

Architectural historian Adrian Forty, in defining a type of transparency which he calls "transparency of meaning," quotes Susan Sontag: "transparence

FIGURE 3.14 Rendering of Friedrichstrasse Skyscraper project by Mies van der Rohe (1921), Berlin-Mitte, Germany. Perspective of northeast corner shows a high-rise with façades draped in frameless glass panels against the silhouettes of thin floor slabs.

© The Museum of Modern Art/Licensed by SCALA/Art Resource, NY.

means experiencing the luminousness of the thing in itself, of things being what they are."[21] Forty writes that this idea – that the meaning of a work is in the sensory experience of the thing itself – was a core ideal of modern art and architecture. Early glass buildings by Mies were thought to embody the meaning of transparency, with glass skins hung from a steel skeleton, clearly revealing the tectonic means in ways strikingly different from opaque masonry walls.

With the Willis Building, Foster realizes Mies's dream of frameless glass panels suspended from concrete slabs; the newly developed curtain wall system "reduced the major elements down to just glass and glue," says Foster.[22] In doing so, the building materializes transparency of meaning, revealing the tectonics of a glass curtain suspended from a concrete floor slab. Working with glass manufacturer Pilkington, Foster developed the system with yacht designer Martin Francis and structural engineer Tony Hunt. Pilkington had an existing all-glass system, but it was ground-supported, and therefore not usable for

FIGURE 3.15 Glass Skyscraper project by Mies van der Rohe. View of lost model. No intended site known (1922). The irregularly shaped, amoeba-like plan is suggestive of the Willis Building's implied curves.

Digital image © The Museum of Modern Art/Licensed by SCALA/Art Resource, NY.

a three-story building. The manufacturer was also developing a suspended system using tempered glass with steel patch plates and silicon joints, but only for a single-story, straight-run building. The Willis Building presented the challenges of a faceted façade, which required the corner patches to accommodate glass meeting at numerous angles. The tinted glass also required tempering which, at the time, presented technical problems. A backup for an all-glass curtain wall was an existing system by Modern Art Glass, which would have created visual obstructions; it had tubular steel mullions to provide lateral support and vertical stainless steel and neoprene strips at the joints to secure the glass in place and provide weather seals.[23] Even though numerous presentation renderings of the Willis Building show a curtain wall with vertical mullions (Figure 3.16), the design team's goal was to eliminate mullions as much as possible.[24]

FIGURE 3.16 An early rendering showing a curtain wall scheme with vertical mullions. Façades of neighboring buildings are seen reflected on the curtain wall.

Courtesy of Norman Foster Foundation (1971–1975).

After several months of development, the team succeeded in building an all-glass curtain wall with no mullions. Nine hundred and thirty sheets of glass hung like curtains from the top slab, suspended from a central bolt at the top of the uppermost panel (Figure 3.17). Crafting the enclosure like a curtain reflects Semper's theory of *Bekleidungsprinzip*, or "principal of dressing." Semper's four elements of architecture included enclosure (or cladding), hearth, roof, and mound. His assertion of textile and weaving as the origin of architectural cladding influenced early modern architects, including Otto Wagner in Vienna and Ödön Lechner in Budapest, who draped their buildings in decorative textile-like stone panels.[25] The idea was further applied by Chicago architects for the early curtain walls, and the glass detailing of the Willis Building reflects their influences. Like a curtain track, a clamping strip spreads the load across the top edge of the panel from the center. Corner patch fittings connect the panel to those immediately above and below (Figure 3.18). To accommodate the building's faceted façade, the standard plate is modified to an open

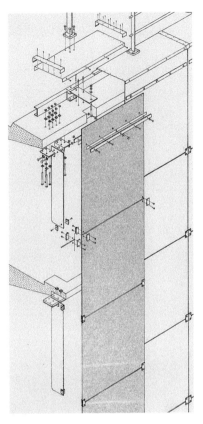

FIGURE 3.17 Sheets of glass hang like curtains from the top slab, suspended from a central bolt at the top of the uppermost panel.

Courtesy of Norman Foster Foundation (1971–1975).

hinge. Half-story glass fins (Figures 3.19 and 3.20) attached to the underside of the concrete floors provide lateral support against horizontal loads, including wind. Patch fittings connect the fins to the glass panels at ninety degrees, with bolts designed to slide vertically to permit movement. Pilkington, though initially skeptical, was persuaded by Foster and Francis's extensive research; the manufacturer eventually agreed to assume full responsibility for design and installation in exchange for a patent on the patch fitting glass system.[26]

The narrow winding streets that surround the Willis Building, combined with the façade's distorted reflections resembling carnival mirrors, can disorient motorists. A driver can quickly become confused as to whether an oncoming car is real or a reflection, or if a car seen on glass is coming or going. As of 2019, three cars have hit the glass façade, but all of them stopped at the line of

FIGURE 3.18 A corner patch plate with bolts captures the corners of four glass panels, drilled with a hole in the corner. The vertical hinge at the center allows faceted glass panels to meet at an angle.

Photograph: Author (2019).

glass, never breaking or penetrating the glass.[27] When a bus collided with the building, the glass moved three inches over five panels, which were pushed back in place by releasing the corner plate bolts. Pilkington's curtain wall system has proven to be robust.

Mies's curvilinear Glass Skyscraper model photograph shows the surrounding masonry buildings reflected on the glass at the base of the skyscraper. A caricature by Sergius Ruegenberg, a Russian architect who worked for Mies, captures Mies stooping down to the street level of his skyscraper model to examine the perceptual effects of glass.[28] As Detlef Mertins writes, Mies's concerns for perceptual effects of materials distanced him from other rationalists. His skyscrapers resonate across a spectrum of architects, from the most rational architects interested in new

FIGURE 3.19 Half-story glass fins attached to the underside of the concrete floor provide lateral support against horizontal loads.

Photograph: Author (2019).

technologies, to those concerned with artists' free expression and visual effects.[29] Mies would most certainly have imagined how the concave and convex faces of the continuous curve would reflect upon each other, where a building's refection on the glass becomes mirrored by another. He may also have foreseen the vertiginous effects of the dynamic, superimposed reflections of oncoming traffic on the curved façades. These effects that can be gleaned from Mies's models and drawings are observed on the façades of the Willis Building. On the concave sections, the reflection of a car approaching perpendicularly to the wall is seen as if it is driving parallel to the building. Once the car passes by, its rear is seen mirrored on the glass, unexpectedly leaping from one glass panel to another. As night falls and the dark glass appears to gradually dematerialize and reveals the office interior and mechanical equipment to the street, reflections of surrounding buildings become merged with the equipment (Figure 3.21). The Willis Building

FIGURE 3.20 Connection of a glass fin to the underside of the concrete floor. Bolts are designed to slide vertically to permit movement.

Photograph: Author (2019).

achieves a complex overlapping of spaces, times, and programs that Mies likely imagined by lowering his head to examine his frameless glass skyscraper models, effects that differ from those of his Lake Shore Drive or the Seagram Building with visible steel mullions.

Influence of the Willis Building on Recent Glass Curtain Walls

The collaborative realization of a frameless curtain wall became a foundation for Foster's future work with manufacturers and engineers to develop previously untested glass details. He continues to push the technical limits of glass construction, completing notable glass buildings including the Reichstag addition in Berlin (1999), the Great Court of the British Museum (2000), and the Swiss Re Tower in London (2004). Moreover, the Willis Building challenged

FIGURE 3.21 Photos of the southwest side taken about an hour apart during dusk. The mechanical equipment on the ground floor slowly becomes revealed as the light inside becomes brighter than the exterior light, and the reflections of surrounding buildings become merged with the equipment.

Photograph: Author (2019).

the natural skepticism for frameless curtain walls, giving confidence to glass engineers and architects; its glass details became an impetus for a multitude of frameless curtain wall types. Martin Francis, a key collaborator on the Willis curtain wall and a member of Foster's office for 20 years, co-founded Rice Francis Ritchie (RFR) with structural engineer Peter Rice and architect Ian Ritchie. RFR would become renowned for their suspended glass system using a two or four-point bolt connection commonly known as the "spider" fittings. In 1981, RFR began collaborating on the suspended glass wall of the three Serres (greenhouses) along the exterior of the Cité des Sciences et de l'Industrie by Adrien Fainsilber at the Parc de la Villette in Paris (Figure 3.22). The architect referenced the Willis Building's state of the art glass technology and proposed transparent rectangular volumes that serve as transition zones between the park and the museum. The wall comprises a two-meter square grid of glass panels suspended by four-point fittings attached to cable trusses, which are

FIGURE 3.22 Serres at Cité des Sciences et de l'Industrie (1986) by Adrien Fainsilber, Paris.

Photograph: Carl Campbell.

tensioned against steel columns. The system accommodates greater movement in distance and angles than the Willis Building's bolted glass panels, which are attached to a relatively rigid concrete frame. Peter Rice credits the Willis Building for the "know-how and the confidence necessary for suspended structural glass system."[30] The bolted suspension system was further applied to the Louvre Pyramid (1989) and would become a symbol of high-tech glass architecture in the 1990s.

The perception of glass at the Serres differs from that of the Willis Building. The glass planes of the latter are made legible from the interior by the silicone joints and the reflective edges of the vertical glass fins. When viewing out from the interior of the Serres's suspension system, the glass planes are defined by the series of points and lines of the metal fittings; the glass sheets by contrast are dematerialized by light shining in from the outside (Figure 3.23). When viewing from the outside in daytime, in both buildings the glass becomes visibly present by the reflections captured on the smooth surfaces. At both Serres and the Louvre Pyramids, the hardware of the suspension system visually dominates and, in some ways, makes the buildings less transparent. The glass and reflections appear to fall to the background, while the eyes are drawn to the dense field of jewel-like, precisely machined and polished metal hardware. By comparison, the patch plates of the Willis Building are finished in matte dark gray to merge with the glass tint and allow the effects on the glass to be foregrounded. The Willis Building has had an undeniable influence on the *Grand Projets* under François Mitterrand, as well as on other High Tech architecture worldwide.

FIGURE 3.23 Serres at Cité des Sciences et de l'Industrie (1986) by Adrien Fainsilber, Paris. When viewing out from the interior of the suspension system, the glass planes are defined by the series of points and lines of the metal fittings.

Hugh Dutton Associés.

Buckminster Fuller and Climatroffice

If Mies's glass skyscrapers partly inspired Foster to design a frameless curtain wall, Buckminster Fuller's thinking on shelter, energy, and environment impressed Foster to rethink the architecture of workspace as well as the sustainability, long before it became mainstream.[31] Foster and Fuller met in 1971 when Fuller was looking for a collaborator on the Samuel Becket Theatre in Oxford. During their first encounter, their ideas on design, materials, and research resonated so well that Fuller selected Foster. For the next 13 years, they collaborated on four projects and stayed close friends.[32] Throughout his career, Foster has attributed his inspirations for sustainability and the unorthodox geometric forms of his buildings to his mentor and friend "Bucky" Fuller. He writes, "he was not simply a technocrat visionary, but the very essence of a moral conscience, forever warning about the fragility of the planet and man's responsibility to protect it."[33] For Foster, each project is a response to the challenges Fuller set out for him as a young architect, and the Willis Building was one of the first projects influenced by Fuller's ideas.

With Dome over Midtown of 1960 (Figure 3.24), Fuller proposed to cover Midtown Manhattan along 42nd Street with a two-mile wide glass-enclosed geodesic dome. At such distance, the dome's structural members would be invisible from the street, minimizing visual obstructions. New Yorkers would be protected from the elements, yet be visually connected to the sky and the rivers. Enclosed by a shell thick enough to be occupied between sheets of glass, Fuller claimed that the dome would save the city the costs of air-

FIGURE 3.24 Dome over Midtown (1960) by Buckminster Fuller.
Courtesy of The Estate of R. Buckminster Fuller.

conditioning, street cleaning, and snow removal.[34] Fuller readily admitted that the idea of building a collectively shared dome in Manhattan, where land owners battle over air rights, would be improbable.[35] He made the proposition before the oil crisis of the 1970s, the point at which heating and cooling costs would render the scheme even more unlikely.

The Dome over Midtown was a foundation for Foster and Fuller's Climatroffice concept of 1971 (Figure 3.25). Climatroffice, their second collaboration following the theatre, featured multilevel office floors with a bank of escalators in the center, and enclosed by an oval glass dome which housed offices and shared gardens in a controlled microclimate.[36] Foster remarked that Climatroffice was a vision for "an architecture of interiorized buildings, which live within an envelope so diaphanous that its presence is perceived as being closer to the sky or clouds than any conventional structure."[37] Both the Dome and the Climatroffice aimed to bring "nature and the workspace together within a lightweight flexible enclosure."[38] Fuller developed ideas for lightweight glazed domes, such as the Montreal Expo geodesic dome and the St. Louis Climatron. Likewise, Foster's early sketches for the Willis Building show a lightweight transparent shell with flexible office floors. The building realizes ideas latent in Climatroffice.

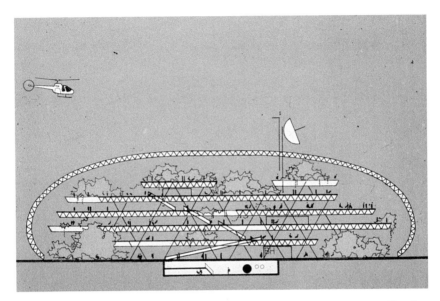

FIGURE 3.25 Climatroffice (1971) by Norman Foster and Buckminster Fuller featured multilevel office floors with a bank of escalators in the center, enclosed by an oval glass dome which housed offices and shared gardens.

Courtesy of Norman Foster Foundation.

Foster has designed multiple iterations of a glass dome as a workspace that brings nature inside. They have been met with both praise and criticism. The most recent example is the Apple Park, a ring-shaped headquarters building with 2.5 million square feet of office space in the suburb of Cupertino. Called an "anachronism wrapped in glass"[39] by *Wired* magazine, it is a high-tech glass bubble – with a toroid glass roof and curved, frameless glass walls – isolated in the suburbs away from where most employees live. Using glass, a material firmly intertwined with Apple's products and corporate image, Jobs and Foster aimed to create an innovation campus for the next century. However, architects, technologists, and employees remain critical of an office in a bubble that is notoriously secretive and opaque in office policies. The idea of a life in a suburban bubble is satirized in the science fiction *Truman Show* (1998) in which the main character Truman Burbank lives his life, unbeknownst to himself, in a giant stage set covered by a semispherical dome. His family and friends are all actors, and the weather and events are all artificially created. In many ways, life in a bubble remains associated with artificiality, particularly when situated in a nonurban environment like Cupertino. The critique that such an office environment is an anachronism is accurate, since the idea of an open office stems from the late 1950s.

Climatroffice was preceded by about a decade of growing interest in *Büro-landschaft* ("office landscape" in German), an organic office layout developed from 1958 by Quickborner, a German consulting company. Quickborner, founded by two sons of a furniture designer, offered an organically laid out open floor office as an alternative to closed-door, hierarchical private cubicles. *Bürolandschaft* motivated Herman Miller to design, also in 1958, lines of modular furniture which continue to spawn a variety of open-layout, adaptable furniture today. Rendering of Climatroffice by Foster's office (Figure 3.26) shows an office furniture system with partitions, in a sky-lit open office with a green floor finish that matches the colors of plants growing in the office and on the roof. From the idea of Climatroffice developed with Fuller to the notion of *Bürolandschaft*, Willis Building materialized an agglomeration of ideas budding in the 1960s and 70s concerning democratic, transparent office culture. At a scale of architectural practice and projects matched by only a few, if any, of

FIGURE 3.26 Climatroffice (1971) by Norman Foster and Buckminster Fuller. The drawing shows an office furniture system with partitions, in a sky-lit open office with a green floor finish that matches the colors of plants growing among desks and on the roof.

Courtesy of Norman Foster Foundation.

his peers, Foster has continued to translate Fuller's seemingly implausible visions of thin glass membranes into buildings.

Innovative Mechanical Systems

The fundamental link between glass architecture and the problem of heating and cooling was recognized by both Le Corbusier and Paul Scheerbart. Le Corbusier proposed his "neutralizing wall," or double glass wall that would counteract heat loss and gain.[40] He proposed a double façade for the competition entries of the League of Nations in Geneva and the Salvation Army City of Refuge in Paris, and implemented it at the Tsentrosoyuz office building (1929–1935) in Moscow. Scheerbart's writing likewise advocated double glass walls, prophetically writing that double glass walls spaced a meter or more apart will be an essential condition in all glass architecture.[41] Similar to other glass buildings with extraordinary transparency, including SANAA's Glass Pavilion in Toledo, the reading of the Willis Building's transparency is dependent on the integration of mechanical, electrical, and plumbing systems into the architecture. While a single glazing system may seem at odds with contemporary ideas of sustainability, the building was energy efficient for its time. This was achieved by keeping the building perimeter, where the temperature fluctuates, largely unoccupied by furniture. Instead, the perimeter zone was kept open for circulation and impromptu gatherings. Additionally, the roof garden with a deep layer of soil provided insulation from heat gain and loss. When the building was completed in 1975, the company did not have desktop computers; instead, a mainframe computer occupied an entire separate computer suite. Within a decade, the company introduced computers at individual desks. Foster's office anticipated the need for electrical flexibility and incorporated a raised floor for IT wiring, long before desktop computers became the norm. When computers were installed at each desk, the building was able to accommodate them with minimal disruption to the workflow and avoid visually obstructive cable trays or channels.

A variety of anticipatory moves by the design team enabled the building to continue to perform its intended functions. Both architects and clients take a risk in failure and obsolescence when they innovate with building systems or materials. With the Willis Building, the architecture has withstood and adapted to nearly five decades of rapid transformations in energy code, information technology, and workplace culture. Although a single-layer glass curtain wall of this size would not meet today's energy standards, visionary integration of systems enabled the building to continually adapt to changing needs.

Transparency for Workplaces

The Willis Building transformed a traditional office environment by providing amenities for its employees, such as a swimming pool shared by employees and families after-hours; a rooftop cafeteria with a planted garden; a coffee bar; and a gym. The building is a far-reaching contrast to the 19th century masonry office buildings with relatively small windows, or the *Mad Men* era glass sky-scrapers in which the perimeter window walls are monopolized by the executives, limiting the daylight or views out for other employees. By introducing new types of programs and material choices, the Willis Building redefined what a workplace could offer its employees. These amenities are architecturally celebrated and prominently situated, with glass transparency playing a significant role. The pool is axially located just beyond the central bank of escalators and is visible from the entrance. In section, the surface of the water aligns with the striking green rubber flooring of the lobby, as if to suggest one could walk across the reflective surface of the water.[42] Transparency is also at play in a recreational area. Through the glass wrapping the pool deck, the swimmers view into the carefully curated and illuminated mechanical equipment, and watch the cars driving to and from the roundabout of Franciscan Way and Princes Street.

From the lobby, the escalators ascend to the glass-enclosed restaurant on the roof level (Figure 3.27), from which employees can walk onto grass to take breaks on the lawn while taking in panoramic views of the historic city. The green colored finishes of the interior mirror the color of the grass on the roof, as though the lawn is seamlessly pulled into the office floors through the glass enclosure of the restaurant; materializing the idea of the "landscape office." Inside, the material choices invert the conventions; the reception, normally the area that receives the most luxurious material finishes, has a paint finish and a utilitarian raised coin rubber flooring, whereas the office floors have carpets and custom-designed ceiling systems that integrate lighting, air, smoke detectors, and sprinklers.[43]

The idea of a new workplace had previously been envisioned by Frank Lloyd Wright at the Larkin Building (1903). Wright designed the building to enhance productivity and morale of the employees by providing air-conditioning, a dining room, and a lounge with a fireplace.[44] However, the layout fostered hierarchy by allowing supervisors to oversee the workers from above. In contrast, the Willis Building removes hierarchical walls and supervision sight lines; doors are nearly nonexistent, creating a radically open work environment. The Willis Building also differs from the suburban low-rise office buildings clad in reflective glass. Reinhold Martin, in his book *The Organizational Complex*, theorizes the corporate glass buildings built in the United States after World War II, arguing that the curtain wall systems deployed by these companies mirrored the systems of the corporate organizations housed inside.[45] Often situated in suburban corporate parks, these mirrored glass buildings reflected a sea of parking lots, contrasting the medley of buildings and active streetscapes captured on the Willis Building's glass walls.

FIGURE 3.27 From the roof level, the entrance lobby can be seen through the central sky-lit atrium.

Photograph: Author (2019).

While planted roofs have lately become abundant in sustainable design, in the early 1970s, turfed roofs on high-tech glass buildings were not prevalent. Reyner Banham calls the coupling of the turfed roof with a high-tech glass building a "shot-gun marriage without apology."[46] The Willis Building's planted roof with a restaurant was influenced by landscape architect Ralph Hancock's former roof garden (1935) atop the Derry and Toms Department Store (1933) in central London. This Art Deco building's rooftop garden, which remained highly popular until its closing in 2018, was kept invisible from the street. Only upon ascent to the roof, did visitors encounter the fantastic Spanish Garden with Moorish pergola and the English Tudor Garden with follies and fountains. Similarly, the fourth-floor restaurant and roof garden of the Willis Building are not readily apparent from the street. Their presence are hinted at by the trimmed hedges that line the roof perimeter along the metal tube guardrails. Upon ascending the escalators to the top floor, through the cafeteria, the green lawn of the roof becomes visible as an accessible social space. Instead of sitting among pergolas and follies, Willis employees taking a break on the roof are seated at a picnic table situated between a mechanical duct and a vent, all painted black, as if they were minimalist sculptures, or a Corbusian ocean liner (Figure 3.28). This inversion to expose mechanical systems, which have conventionally been concealed, is revisited in many British High Tech buildings, including Richard Rogers (Foster's classmate at Yale) and Renzo Piano's Pompidou Center in Paris – designed and constructed nearly concurrently with the Willis Building – and the Lloyd's building (1986) in London by Rogers. Glass transparency at the Willis Building transforms the culture of offices space by artfully exposing the "organs" of the building, removing

FIGURE 3.28 Exposed mechanical duct and a vent on the roof, with a black picnic table in between.

Photograph: Author (2019).

private offices and obstacles along exterior glass walls, and placing employee amenities where they are most visible from the streets and the central circulation space.

Merging Past Dreams with Anticipated Future

The Willis Building realizes the dream of frameless curtain walls depicted in Mies's drawings from the 1920s. As foreshadowed in drawings, the Willis Building's legibility depends on the interplay of reflected light, as well as the contrast of light behind and in front of glass. Unlike the earlier modern glass buildings such as the Zonnestraal in which glass fills apertures framed by concrete, the Willis Building is sheathed almost entirely in glass, which both shields and reveals the concrete structure beyond. Depending upon the light conditions, the building offers contrasting readings of both a monolithic black mass and a gossamer veil draped upon a concrete frame. Like Mies's 1921 Friedrichstrasse competition entry high-rise that dramatically stands out from the historic city, the Willis Building distinguishes itself from the rest of Ipswich by seemingly eliminating the cornice, plinth, and human-scale details that the neighboring buildings posses . In this seeming dismissal of the historic context, the Willis Building asserts a contextualism rooted in the footsteps of medieval times. It allows the winding medieval paths to shape its volumes and presents a living panorama of Ipswich on its frameless glass screen. Concurrently, it looked ahead of its time to establish new standards for a democratic workspace and glass curtain walls that would be emulated for decades to follow.

Notes

1 Foster Associates was co-founded by Wendy and Norman Foster in 1967, following the dissolution of Team 4, a partnership with Su and Richard Rogers. In 1999, the firm name was shortened to Foster + Partners.
2 Norman Foster and Kenneth Powell, *Willis Faber & Dumas Headquarters: Foster + Partners* (Munich: Prestel, 2013), 10.
3 "Our history," Willis Towers Watson, accessed August 30, 2019, www.willistowers watson.com/en-US/about-us/our-history.
4 Foster and Powell, *Willis Faber & Dumas Headquarters*, 14.
5 Foster and Powell, *Willis Faber & Dumas Headquarters*, 15.
6 Foster and Powell, *Willis Faber & Dumas Headquarters*, 24.
7 Foster and Powell, *Willis Faber & Dumas Headquarters*, 14–21.
8 Malcolm Quantrill, *The Norman Foster Studio: Consistency through Diversity* (London: E & FN Spon, 1999), 78–79.
9 Foster and Powell, *Willis Faber & Dumas Headquarters*, 60.
10 Henry N. Cobb, *Henry N. Cobb Words & Works: 1948–2018: Scenes from a Life in Architecture* (New York: Monacelli, 2018), 130.
11 Gordon Cullen, *Townscape* (New York: Reinhold, 1961), 9.
12 Reyner Banham, "Grass above, Glass around," in Mary Banham, Ed., *A Critic Writes: Essays by Reyner Banham* (Berkeley, CA: University of California Press, 1996), 211.
13 Foster and Powell, *Willis Faber & Dumas Headquarters*, 24.

14 Foster and Powell, *Willis Faber & Dumas Headquarters*, 24–25.

15 Foster and Powell, *Willis Faber & Dumas Headquarters*, 28.

16 Peter Page, a facility manager at the Willis Building, interview by author, Ipswich, June 18, 2019. Willis has been the only occupant of the building since 1975 and has never rented space.

17 Foster and Powell, *Willis Faber & Dumas Headquarters*, 28.

18 Page, interview.

19 Rosemarie Haag Bletter, "The Interpretation of the Glass-Dream Expressionist Architecture and the History of the Crystal Metaphor," *Journal of the Society of Architectural Historians* 40, no. 1 (March, 1981), 41.

20 Bletter, "The Interpretation of the Glass-Dream Expressionist Architecture," 41.

21 Adrian Forty, *Words and Buildings: A Vocabulary of Modern Architecture* (London: Thames & Hudson, 2000), 288.

22 Foster and Powell, *Willis Faber & Dumas Headquarters*, 34.

23 Foster and Powell, *Willis Faber & Dumas Headquarters*, 30.

24 Gabriele Bramante and Foster Associates, *Willis Faber & Dumas Building* (London: Phaidon, 1993).

25 Kate Holliday, "Unraveling the Textile in Modern Architecture: Guest Editor's Introduction," *Studies in the Decorative Arts* 16, no. 2 (Spring–Summer, 2009), 2–6.

26 Foster and Powell, *Willis Faber & Dumas Headquarters*, 34.6t5.

27 Page, interview.

28 Detlef Mertins, *Mies* (London: Phaidon, 2013), 70.

29 Mertins, *Mies*, 70.

30 Peter Rice and Hugh Dutton, *Structural Glass* (London: E & FN Spon, 1995), 44.

31 Norman Foster, "Blueprint for the 21st Century," *Modern Painters* 20, no. 5 (2008), 74–79.

32 Foster, "Blueprint for the 21st Century," 74–75.

33 Foster, "Blueprint for the 21st Century," 75.

34 John McHale, *R. Buckminster Fuller* (New York: George Braziller, 1962), plate 102 caption.

35 Ezra Bookstein, *Smith Tapes: Lost Interviews with Rock Stars & Icons 1969–1972* (New York: Princeton Architectural Press, 2015).

36 Foster, "Blueprint for the 21st Century," 76.

37 Foster and Powell, *Willis Faber & Dumas Headquarters*, 54.

38 Foster and Powell, *Willis Faber & Dumas Headquarters*, 19.

39 Adam Rogers, "If You Care about Cities, Apple's New Campus Sucks," *Wired* online, last modified June 8, 2017, accessed July 5, 2019, www.wired.com/story/apple-campus/.

40 Le Corbusier, Paul Stirton, and Tim Benton, "Glass, the Fundamental Material of Modern Architecture," *West 86th: A Journal of Decorative Arts, Design History, and Material Culture* 19, no. 2 (Fall–Winter, 2012), 287.

41 Paul Scheerbart and Bruno Taut, *Glass Architecture, by Paul Scheerbart; and Alpine Architecture, by Bruno Taut* ed. Dennis Sharp (New York: Praeger, 1972), 42.

42 Foster and Powell, *Willis Faber & Dumas Headquarters*, 57. The pool was decked over in 1991 to make room for additional desks. It was done in a reversible manner so that it could be used as a pool again should the company decide to in the future.

43 Foster and Powell, *Willis Faber & Dumas Headquarters*, 48.

44 "Larkin Company Administration Building," Frank Lloyd Wright Trust, accessed July 10, 2019, https://flwright.org/researchexplore/wrightbuildings/larkincompanyadministrationbuilding.

45 Reinhold Martin, *The Organizational Complex* (Cambridge, MA: MIT Press, 2003).

46 Banham, "Grass above, Glass around," 210.

4

CRACKING THE GLASS CEILING OF A CRYSTAL PALACE

The Jacob K. Javits Convention Center

When Hillary Clinton accepted her 2016 presidential party's nomination, she announced that the Democrats "just put the biggest crack in that *glass ceiling*"[1] (italics added by author for emphasis). On the days leading to the election, journalists remarked that she would spend the election night under the largest glass ceiling in New York City, the Jacob K. Javits Convention Center by I. M. Pei and Partners (Figures 4.1 and 4.2). The architects' inspiration for this 410,000 square-foot convention center made of steel space frame and sheathed in glass was Crystal Palace, an exhibit hall commissioned by Prince Albert to showcase Great Britain's achievements and potentials in free trade. A monumental feat of prefabricated construction, Crystal Palace was designed by Joseph Paxton. Paxton was a greenhouse designer of modest background who, with his boundless imagination and propensity for efficiency and spectacle, rose through the ranks to win the admirations of the British nobility. In Victorian England, glass conservatories, by which Paxton's design of Crystal Palace was directly influenced, were associated with republican ideals. With light entering the building from every direction, glass pavilions left no one space privileged.[2] Isobel Armstrong, a scholar of literary and cultural criticism, in her book *Victorian Glassworlds* asserts that the 20th century conservatory, also known as a nursery and a forcing house (for creating hybrid species), was "predicated on violence and nurture, beauty and coercion."[3] Tellingly, from its conception, the Javits Center was associated with the exhibition of objects and people, civic ideals, and the duality of beauty and coercion.

Clinton's loss subsequently generated various uses of this metaphor, including "Highest glass ceiling remains intact after Clinton's stunning loss,"[4] and "cracked, but intact."[5] Crystals and glass have historically been associated with spiritual, personal, and social metamorphosis.[6] Clinton's team appropriated the

FIGURE 4.1 Interior of the Jacob K. Javits Convention Center by I. M. Pei and Partners.

Photograph: Thorney Lieberman. Pei, Cobb, Freed and Partners (1986).

story of her transformation to a crystalline building. Furthermore, the election night's suspense, enchantment, and near-triumph of the disadvantaged are all elements of fairy tales, which describe the collective dreams of a culture. This chapter examines the social, material, and cultural intertwining in the glass ceiling metaphor. An analysis of the material properties of glass, the technical advancement in recent years, and the cultural context of fictions offer complex readings of this metaphor.

The Glass Ceiling Metaphor

The Glass Ceiling figure of speech was first introduced into the mainstream by *The Wall Street Journal* in an article published on March 24, 1986. It read, "Even those few women who rose steadily through the ranks eventually crashed into an invisible barrier. The executive suite seemed within their grasp, but they just couldn't break through the glass ceiling"[7] (Figure 4.3). The origin of this metaphor is traced to a presentation at the 1978 Women at Work Exposition held

FIGURE 4.2 Photographed day view along 11th Avenue. During the day, the glass reflects the surrounding buildings, appearing dark, and near opaque.

Photograph: Thorney Lieberman. Pei, Cobb, Freed and Partners (1986).

in Manhattan. The presenter, Marilyn Loden, was an internal organization development consultant for the Bell Telephone System, a company whose switchboard operators were almost all women.[8] Since 1974, she had managed an executive development program called the Male–Female Awareness Workshop to bring awareness of sexism in the workplace and to better integrate women into management positions. At the 1978 exposition, she spoke on a panel named Mirror, Mirror on the Wall, a title which suggests narcissism and notably references the words of the evil queen in *Snow White*. She heard one woman after another express, in self-deprecating ways, that "women were inadequately socialized for success and limited their own career aspirations due to low self-esteem."[9] The repeated attention to the weaknesses of women's leadership styles became exasperating. Prompted by the mirror reference in the panel title, she asserted, without a prepared speech: "While low self-esteem might be an issue for a few, the 'invisible glass ceiling,' i.e., the barriers to advancement that were organizational not personal, was having a much greater impact on women's career aspirations".[10]

FIGURE 4.3 Article by Carol Hymowitz and Timothy D. Schellhardt, "The glass ceiling: Why women can't seem to break the invisible barrier that blocks them from the top jobs."

The Wall Street Journal, March 24, 1986, 61.

Her introduction of this architectural metaphor accomplished two goals central to the issues of women's professional advancement. First, instead of placing the blame on a particular group of people (i.e. insecure women or chauvinistic men), by using a material metaphor, the problem – the elusive, yet clearly present barrier – took on a nonhuman identity. Second, by asserting that underrepresentation of women was largely an external, cultural problem, it was no longer seen as exclusively an internal problem for women to solve by altering their behaviors or appearances.

Both Loden's presentation in 1978 and her book *Feminine Leadership, or How to Succeed in Business Without Being One of the Boys* (1985)[11] presented an alternative outlook on how women could effectively lead in a style different than men; it is "about the future – about potentials and possibilities," she writes, rather than about how feminine traits should be corrected to follow more traditionally masculine approaches. In a 2018 phone interview, she spoke critically of speakers and writers from the past four decades who instructed women to behave and dress more like men, advice insinuating that women were the source of the problem, and that men were the source of model behaviors and appearances.[12] A similar view is evident in the architectural metaphor of "sticky floor," coined by leadership expert Rebecca Shambaugh in her 2007 book *It's Not a Glass Ceiling, It's a Sticky Floor*.[13] Shambaugh argues that while the glass ceiling is an external barrier, similar to the boys' club, that prevents the ascension of women, the barrier is actually "sticky floors." The floor is internal and within reach and, presumably, women have more control to "mop" the floors beneath them. She includes advice such as "forming your own board of directors," "embracing," or being "good enough in your work," as examples of sticky floors issues within women's control.[14]

The metaphors of the sticky floor and the glass ceiling present two different views of the same problem. The former internalizes the obstacle, whereas the latter externalizes it. In contrast to cleaning the sticky floor, breaking the glass ceiling exhibits aspirations for ascension. Realizing the difficulty of breaking the glass barrier appears more bittersweet when one is reaching for the sky. The difference between the two material metaphors also implies issues of class. While corporate women aspire to reach the sky, working-class women are trapped at the floor level. A year after Loden coined the term, Katherine Lawrence of Hewlett-Packard publicized it at an annual conference of the Women's Institute for Freedom of the Press. She said: "I presented the concept of how in corporate America, the official policy is one way – the sky's the limit – but in actuality, the sky had a glass ceiling for women."[15]

By 1991, this trope took on the authority of law, when Title II of the Civil Rights Act of 1991 created the "Glass Ceiling Commission" by the Department of Labor, which published its results in 1995. It investigated how to make "solid investments" to "dismantle" the glass ceiling.[16]

Rather than an opaque building material such as wood, concrete, or steel, glass was selected for its seemingly invisible quality. Women's skyward ascension appears to be within reach, but a clear yet impenetrable barrier stands between them and their destinations. Glass suggests a barrier that is not readily visible from afar, as concrete or steel would be. The physical barrier, however, is clearly present. The 1986 "Glass Ceiling" article from *The Wall Street Journal* says: "Corporate women say most of the discrimination they encounter is subtle, even unconscious."[17] Women might suddenly find their path blocked by a transparent wall that is hard to anticipate. As the article says, "Bumping the glass ceiling can be excruciatingly painful, especially for women who were early pioneers in their fields."[18] As *The Guardian*'s Zoe Williams wrote a day after Clinton's nomination acceptance at the 2016 Democratic National Convention, the thin glass barrier appears to be so subtle that "those who pass through it refuse to recognize" its presence.[19] Moreover, a property of glass is that once broken, it remains broken. If the metaphorical glass ceiling's behavior were true to the physical material's properties, she argues, then the ceiling that Sheryl Sandberg shattered would have left the ceiling wide open for others to follow.[20] On the contrary, the glass ceiling appears to self-heal as soon as a woman shatters it.

When Marilyn Loden coined the phrase "glass ceiling," she was not conscious of modern glass building's association with the future, optimism, or ascension. On the contrary, she had in mind a more negative association with the material; she invoked glass to describe a barrier that is invisible, but present and impenetrable.[21] Glass can deceive; its properties belie its initial appearance. The metaphor is apt for women gazing upward and aspiring to ascend the corporate ladder. The vertical organization of corporate management charts that locate executives at the top are spatialized in corporate office buildings, where the chief executives occupy the highest floor. Height is linked to authority and power. Accordingly, the glass ceiling seals out women and others who are underrepresented; they are kept just beneath the level to which they aspire. In the field of economics, price ceilings and price floors are controls put in place by the government when they believe a good or service is being sold for too high or low a price, respectively. In other words, ceilings are externally placed limits, a form of control. Analogously, a glass ceiling is placed upon women by the government, corporations, or other authorities to control women's rise in society.

Ceilings and Glass Transparency in Architecture

Architects have written on the distinction in meaning between the upward and downward gaze. Gottfried Semper wrote that, in good taste, the floor should not have too much decoration as it will draw the eye downward, whereas light ornamentation of the ceiling will "draw the eye upward by the colors that are airy, light and at the same time restful."[22] He wrote that the ceiling should, as the "climax of the effect [...] exceed the decoration of the walls in its splendor."[23]

In modern architecture, glass is often associated with optimism and future. Paul Scheerbart envisioned a utopic future filled with crystalline glass buildings. In his 1914 book *Glasarchiteckur*, he wrote:

> If we want our culture to rise to a higher level, we are obliged [...] to change our architecture. And this only becomes possible if we take away the closed character from the rooms in which we live. We can only do that by introducing glass architecture, which lets in the light of the sun, the moon, and the stars, not merely through a few windows, but through every possible wall, which will be made entirely of glass [...][24]

For Scheerbart and his German Expressionist colleagues, glass-crystal symbolized a newly transformed society. Rosemarie Haag Bletter writes that they chose glass for its malleability while in the molten state, and for its "extraordinarily unstable conception of architecture" resulting from its shimmering, illusory reflections.[25]

In the late 20th and 21st centuries, the transparency of glass has often been appropriated to symbolize openness, accessibility, and freedom. Glass in the Louvre Pyramid by I. M. Pei and the Reichstag renovation in Berlin by Norman Foster are often associated with democratic government. The Louvre Pyramid was commissioned by François Mitterrand to symbolize the transparency of the French government. However, as Annette Fierro contends, the transparency of Pei's glass *Grande Pyramide* conflicts with this alleged institutional transparency: there is a discrepancy between the idealized transparency and the physical manifestation of the mirror effect, which makes the glass appear opaque from the outside.[26] Seen from the outside, the relatively darker interior of the lobby reflects the sky and the palace to the viewer. Seen from within, the truss structure just below the glazing surface can obstruct outward.[27] At the Reichstag, the new glass dome was presented by the competition-winning architect as a symbol of democratic ideology for a reunified Germany.[28] The public ascends up the dome to symbolically gaze down – through glass – upon their representatives who assemble in the plenary chamber below. While the view from under the Louvre Pyramid is obstructed by metal structures that support the glass panels, the gaze down towards the representatives also contains structural barriers. The glass that acoustically seals the plenary chamber from the public space above is reflective. The public sees reflections of the dome and themselves looking into the chamber. The interior of the sunlit dome is brighter than the chamber below, making it a challenge to see down into the assembly. The reading of glass transparency is dependent on light conditions on both sides of the glass sheet. Intended symbolism behind glass can also be read or misread depending on its context.

The Jacob K. Javits Convention Center

The Javits Center (1979–1986) was named after Jacob Javits, a Jewish Liberal Republican who served as a New York senator from 1957 to 1981. The architects were I. M. Pei and his partner James Ingo Freed. In an interview, the project architect Perry Chin recalls that it was Pei who first looked to the precedents of the Crystal Palace by Paxton, the Palm House (1844–1848) in Kew Gardens, and the Grand Palais (1897–1900) in Paris.[29] The architect, not the client, chose glass. During study tours of new convention halls around the country, James Freed observed that most of them were dark boxes disconnected from the public. Freed explains, "I wanted to find a tool that capitalized on the exposition side of a convention center, and that prompted light and transparency,"[30] and decided to "provide a direct visual connection to the city."[31] Inspired by Paxton's Crystal Palace, the Javits Center became the country's largest space frame structure, spanning five blocks from 34th to 39th Streets, between 11th and 12th Avenues at the western edge of Manhattan along the Hudson River. Organized by clear north–south and east–west axial circulation paths, it accommodates up to 85,000 people within its exhibition halls, lobbies, banquet halls, offices, cafeterias, and other spaces.[32]

The exhibit hall connects with the city visually, with a cross-axial view of the Empire State Building along 34th Street and a glass-enclosed, indoor promenade called the "galleria" where visitors experience spectacular views of the Hudson River. Despite these views, the Javits Center remained isolated from the city and, for decades, the connection remained only visual. The closest subway stop was three long blocks away at Penn Station, connected by an inconvenient walk through the industrial wasteland of Hell's Kitchen choked with Lincoln Tunnel traffic. The building was criticized for not bolstering the city's relationship to the Hudson River.[33] Because of the then-proposed plans to build an elevated highway along the Hudson River, the Javits largely faced its opaque glass back to the waterfront. In 2014, the completion of the High Line's Phase III brought public attention and foot traffic to the Hudson Yards, a massive commercial, cultural, and residential development immediately south of the Javits Center. In 2015, the number seven train extended to the Hudson Yards stop on 34th Street and 11th Avenue, finally making the Javits easily accessible by subway. Pedestrian traffic on and around the High Line has also increased the visibility of the building, exposing the grand glass hall to public view, as the architects probably imagined, though it occurred only after the Javits Center's original dark gray glass was replaced in 2013 by FXFowle with more transparent glass treated with frit pattern (silk-screened ceramic dots) and higher performance reflective coating.[34]

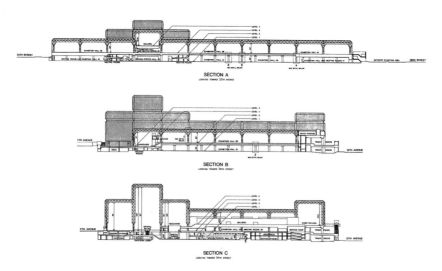

FIGURE 4.4 Longitudinal and transverse sections of the Javits Center. Architects envisioned a building wrapped with a continuous glass roof and walls.

Pei, Cobb, Freed and Partners (1986).

James Freed envisioned a building wrapped with a continuous glass roof and walls (Figure 4.4). This design intent informed the choice of a space frame structure designed with structural engineer Matthys Levy of Weidlinger Associates. Freed explicitly states that the influence came from Paxton's Crystal Palace, not from Buckminster Fuller's work or the British High Tech.[35] Despite Freed's lack of intentional association with Fuller's space frames, it is worth noting the Javit's Center's link to Fuller. The ideas advocated by Fuller – resisting overspecialization and embracing comprehensive and synergetic thinking in order to serve the entire world population – would suggest that the space frame's intentions were to neither control nor oppress but, on the contrary, to liberate people from social norms and gender categorizations.

FIGURE 4.5 10-foot square glass panels attached to the steel space frame on the east façade.

Photograph: ART on FILE.

Even though the glass specification and the space frame details are the same for the horizontal and vertical faces of the building, the project required two separate subcontractors for the glass skin – one for the wall, and a separate skylight contractor who installed and provided warranty for the roof. Today, it is customary for a single façade contractor to take responsibility for both the walls and the roof but, in the early 1980s, an all-glass skin was still unusual, and therefore riskier, for the contractors. The 10-foot grid of glass, in both vision glass and spandrels, gave a continuous reading to the skin all around the building. The expansive east façade (Figure 4.5) made up of 10 x 10 foot monolithic glass presents a view of the Empire State Building on the axis along 34th Street. On the walls above street level and the glass ceiling, the makeup of glass is multilayered (Figure 4.6). In the original glazing, vertical glass comprises 1-inch insulated glass units (IGU): quarter-inch plus half-inch airspace plus quarter-inch glass. The spandrel units have quarter-inch glass with a scrim – a plastic sheet to protect the coating on the second surface, as the coating was, at the time, sensitive to UV light – and 4 inches of insulation behind a metal panel. The sloped glass and skylights have quarter-inch glass with coating on the second surface, a half-inch airspace, and two quarter-inch sheets of glass laminated to comprise the surface of the roof.[36]

In contrast to the pervasive false ceilings of modernism, the Javits Center's glass ceiling is a true ceiling. The fourth surface (the surface facing the interior space) on the laminated inner glass sheet becomes the ceiling while the IGU

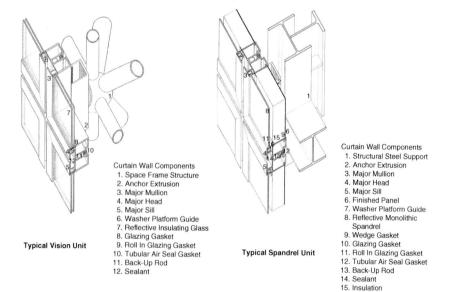

Curtain Wall Components
1. Space Frame Structure
2. Anchor Extrusion
3. Major Mullion
4. Major Head
5. Major Sill
6. Washer Platform Guide
7. Reflective Insulating Glass
8. Glazing Gasket
9. Roll In Glazing Gasket
10. Tubular Air Seal Gasket
11. Back-Up Rod
12. Sealant

Typical Vision Unit

Curtain Wall Components
1. Structural Steel Support
2. Anchor Extrusion
3. Major Mullion
4. Major Head
5. Major Sill
6. Finished Panel
7. Washer Platform Guide
8. Reflective Monolithic
   Spandrel
9. Wedge Gasket
10. Glazing Gasket
11. Roll In Glazing Gasket
12. Tubular Air Seal Gasket
13. Back-Up Rod
14. Sealant
15. Insulation

Typical Spandrel Unit

FIGURE 4.6 Vision glass (left) and spandrel (right) details.

Pei, Cobb, Freed and Partners (1986).

FIGURE 4.7 During the day, the glass reflects the surrounding buildings, appearing dark, and near opaque.

Paul Stevenson Oles/Pei, Cobb, Freed and Partners.

assemblies make up the roof. The word ceiling originated with the necessity to cover the structures of a room, both above and on the sides, as could be done with a coating of plaster.[37] In other words, the ceiling was a thin surface underside of the roof above. Since the 1950s the ceiling has thickened to as much as a few feet deep in order to conceal ducts, pipes, light fixtures, and other infrastructures of modern comfort. Koolhaas writes, "The false ceiling is the sectional equivalent of *poché* – False ceilings are supposed to be meaningless but contain mysteries beyond their banal uniform modular surfaces."[38]

At the Javits Center, the infrastructure normally hidden above the ceiling is moved to the lower levels in order to make the sky visible and bring it closer to the occupants. During the day, the glass reflects the surrounding buildings, appearing dark, and near opaque (Figure 4.7). Illuminated from within at night, the monumental interior becomes visible to the street (Figures 4.8 and 4.9). From the inside, the space frame appears as a delicate lattice structure, evoking the soaring lightness of its inspiration, the Crystal Palace.

The Crystal Palace

The 1851 Crystal Palace was designed for The Great Exhibition of the Works of Industry of All Nations in Hyde Park (Figure 4.10). The earliest building

FIGURE 4.8 Photographed night view of 11th Avenue. Illuminated from within at night, the monumental interior becomes visible to the street. The glass at the street level is uncoated clear glass and so allow views to and from the street.

Photograph: Thorney Lieberman. Pei, Cobb, Freed and Partners (1986).

FIGURE 4.9 Rendered night view of 11th Avenue elevation.

Photograph: Paul Stevenson. Oles/Pei, Cobb, Freed and Partners.

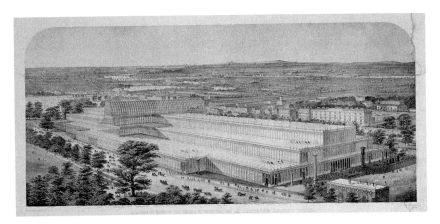

FIGURE 4.10 Aeronautic view of the Great Exhibition Building, the Crystal Palace (1851). Color lithograph by Charles Burton.

Victoria and Albert Museum.

included in the book *Modern Architecture 1851–1945* by Kenneth Frampton and Yukio Futagawa,[39] it is considered by many to signify the beginning of modern architecture for its use of materials and techniques of construction. The stories of its commission and construction read like a "Victorian melo-drama," as told by architectural historian Ralph Lieberman.[40] The triumphal story of the lead designer Joseph Paxton, rising from his humble class origins to become a celebrated designer championed by the British nobility, is suggest-ive of the breaking of a glass ceiling – in his case, an economic class barrier. Neither an architect nor an engineer, Paxton was a son of farmers and a self-taught gardener, who so impressed the Duke of Devonshire with his skills, imagination, and energy that the Duke hired Paxton as the head gardener of Chatsworth. Paxton was sent on global expeditions in the search for new and exotic flora. Over twenty years of experience designing glass greenhouses with wooden structures equipped him with the art of glass detailing, drainage, heat-ing, and ventilation.[41] In 1840, he completed the Great Conservatory of Chatsworth and, in 1850, the Lily House of Chatsworth, built with cast iron columns supporting wooden beams. Inspired by the lily pad structure, it was strong, light, and broad. Prince Albert's Royal Commission had already selected a winning entry for the Great Exhibition hall when the Commission began to question the cost and time span required to build a hall with 17 million bricks. Paxton promised the Commission that he would deliver the entire set of drawings within ten days. His drawings, which he completed in seven days, showed a skeleton of cast iron, wrought iron, and wood (for beams, arches, and gutters), clad with nearly a million square feet of plate glass, prefabricated off-site and erected on site for efficiency. In contrast to the original design that would take significantly longer, Paxton's radically different design was a product of a different ideology.

Isobel Armstrong attributes Paxton's success to "common sense populism,"[42] a designer with an affinity and talent for efficiency, publicity, and persuasion. By comparison, Paxton's rival in conservatory design, John Claudius Loudon, was a scholar and a philosopher who believed that conservatories held civic ideals. To Loudon, a transparent glass dome represented the republican ideal, in which light enters from every direction to create a nonhierarchical space.[43] He also published writings about the civic role of conservatories in society, asserting that they supported the educational duty of the state. Paxton, on the other hand, was more utilitarian, not concerned with the political or cultural debates around the building type. Armstrong highlights the political nature of the conservatory, which was built to keep exotic plants safe in their optimized internal environment irrespective of the seasons and weather (Figure 4.11).

FIGURE 4.11 Great Exhibition Hall of Crystal Palace (1851) by Joseph Paxton in London. Photographic view of interior.

Photograph: Philip Henry Delamotte (1854). Victoria and Albert Museum.

A conservatory manipulates both space and time[44] – by changing temperature, light, and humidity for growing plants, and by accelerating growth. The Great Exhibition of 1851 at the Crystal Palace housed not only trees and plants, but also art, technology, machines, and scientific instruments. Tellingly, the Javits Center's precedent was an exhibition hall designed to create a space for artificially preserving plants and for exhibiting objects. Like its greenhouse predecessors, it was intended to trap heat within a sealed glass shell. Greenhouse, associated with words such as "trap" and "seal," suggests ways to reexamine the social metaphor glass ceiling. The Javit's Center's shed-like organization, delicate steel skeleton clad in glass, and prefabricated construction strategy all have roots in Paxton's Crystal Palace. Moreover, the political significance associated with the Crystal Palace is suggestive of the Clinton campaign's subsequent appropriation of meaning to the Javits Center.

Emergent Properties of Glass

Transparent and fragile in appearance, yet deceptively strong and resistant to breakage, the choice of the material glass as a metaphor for a social barrier is pertinent. The physical qualities of glass increasingly contrast with its appearance. Glass today offers a multitude of visual effects, which were limited in capacity during the mid-20th century: sputtered with reflective metal, insulated with capillary glass, acid etched, sandblasted, laminated with printed interlayers, among many other developments.

In the more than 40 years since the phrase "glass ceiling" was coined in 1978, the profession of architecture has seen significant advances in glass's structural and visual properties. Lamination and thin glass technologies such as SentryGlas® Plus and Gorilla® have made glass far less fragile. SentryGlas®, laminated with ionoplast interlayers and approved by the Miami-Dade County for hurricane resistance,[45] is five times stronger and up to one hundred times stiffer than a conventional polyvinyl butyral (PVB) lamination interlayer.[46] The product is also used where resistance to bullets, blasts, and spalls is desired.

In order to seek new possibilities in glass, architects have worked closely with engineers to challenge the use of glass not only as the envelope, but also as the structure. The Apple Store's five-sided cube on 5th Avenue (2006) in New York is an example that maximizes the transparency and structural properties of glass. This was achieved with a bullet- and hurricane-resistant ionoplast interlayer in the laminated glass roof, structural fins, and wall panels. Moreover, low-iron glass was specified to reduce the green tint of traditional glass and further underscore its transparency. Paradoxically, the more the material appears to disappear, the more unbreakable it becomes.

Gorilla® Glass by Corning is an ultrathin, chemically strengthened glass, made by a fusion-drawn process in which high-purity molten glass is drawn vertically, not horizontally, as is float glass over a molten tin bath.[47] The process is highly pure and precise; the product is untouched by human hands. Once drawn, it is chemically strengthened to create a compressive envelope on the outside that holds it in tension on the inside. Made as thin as 0.4 mm to 2.0 mm in thickness, the most common application of Gorilla® Glass is on smartphone screens and computer displays.[48] The material is clean, smooth, flat, and has an outstanding optical clarity and scratch resistance. Due to its purity, the surfaces have very few imperfections that could cause the glass to go into tension and break.[49] It can be rolled into a tube like a sheet of paper, and it is strong in tension; it belies conventional understanding of the known properties of glass.

Recent technical developments demonstrate that taking hammers to a glass ceiling built with today's break-resistant glass may be sufficient to crack, but not break it. The metaphor is often used to speak of "shattering," "breaking," or "cracking" the glass ceiling. This form of revolution through destruction allows violence to be concentrated on a nonhuman entity, as the Parisians smashed street lanterns – a symbol of the government authority – during the French Revolution.[50] As plastic lamination interlayers become more advanced, increasing the shatter-resistance and stiffness of the glass–plastic laminates, it is the plastic – not glass – that prevents the composite from shattering. Tellingly, in 1991 the Glass Ceiling Commission called for the glass ceiling's "dismantling" as a process of deconstruction.[51] In order to "break" the glass ceiling metaphorically, it appears necessary to disassemble the unbreakable glass in pieces.

In addition to the problem of sealing, glass's brittleness historically presented challenges to its use as a building material. Glass manufacturing and design have advanced to make glass and its assembly components less prone to breakage. As thin and immaterial as it may appear, the glass ceiling is harder to break than opaque false ceilings. Koolhaas writes, "the false celling is always the first victim of a disaster … the building's entrails bursting through the ruptured surface like a hernia."[52] In fact, a significant cause of construction delay at the Javits Center was the cracked steel nodes manufactured by a low-bidding subcontractor who lacked expertise in space frame structures.[53] Steel is perceived to be durable and unbreakable, unlike fragile, delicate glass, but any material can fail when misappropriated, or improperly fabricated.

Advancement in glass construction has not been limited to glass or the plastic interlayer. Transparency is dependent on the appearance and performance of joint sealants between glass panels. Advancements in silicone sealants have enabled glass assemblies to maintain a greater appearance of transparency, while resisting failure. In a cable net glass wall,[54] for example, glass panels are captured at the corners by stainless steel fittings clamped to steel cables tensioned from wall to wall and from the roof to a girder in the floor, with the joints sealed with silicone. The cable net glass wall is designed to deflect wind, analogous to a tennis racquet receiving the force of a moving ball, deflecting up to 22-inches both inward and outward in cases of extreme wind, or a bomb blast.[55] The glass is laminated against breakage; the structural silicone joints are also designed to flex, but not break.

Complex Effects of Glass

Glass as a material conjures an image of transparency, which is presumably what Loden and Lawrence imagined when they chose it as a metaphor for the barrier they found above women. The array of effects now available with glass suggests different scenarios that women may see when they look up towards the glass ceiling from the sealed space below. What is seen on – or through – the glass depends on light's relationship to the glass and the viewer's position. Looking out from inside the Javits Center at night, when the interior is illuminated to levels brighter than the sky, one mainly sees reflections of oneself and the interior, not a view of the sky. The condition is reversed during the day: viewing the building from the exterior, the glass takes on a dark, near-opaque appearance, reflecting the sky, surrounding buildings, and cars.

This reflective property that blurs the Javits Center's presence with its surrounding has had a hazardous effect. Prior to the half-billion-dollar renovation completed in 2013 by FXFowle, the Javits Center had gained notoriety as one of the deadliest buildings for the birds of New York City. Flying birds saw the sky reflected on the glass façade and smashed head-on into it. Their deaths invert the positive associations of glass and reveal its darker side. A team led by FXFowle principle Bruce Fowle, a bird enthusiast, reduced reflectivity and added ceramic frits to make the glass surfaces more visible, decreasing the number of avian deaths by 90%.[56]

As the birds' perception of the building changed with the new glass finish so did the humans'. Through an acid-etched glass ceiling, one can see softened scattered light, but the view above is diffused. This effect is observed in the suspended glass ceiling of Peter Zumthor's Kunsthaus Bregenz (1997). The lantern-like glass volume absorbs the colors of the changing natural light reflected from the sky and from Lake Constance adjacent to the museum. The concrete-bearing structure of this cubic building is concentrated around the perimeter stairs, leaving the central gallery space free of visible columns and beams. The central space is surrounded by vertical and horizontal plenum spaces that allow the flow of light and air. Sunlight is filtered into the gallery through multiple acid-etched glass sheets, first in the vertical walls, then in the horizontal ceilings, to make the galleries glow softly with indirect light. The glass ceiling becomes tinted with the color of the sky but, contrary to expectation, the space beyond is not the sky; above the glass ceiling and the plenum is a concrete floor. The glass ceiling is repeated on three floor levels, topped by a concrete roof. In this building, one sees beyond the luminous ceiling an illusion of the sky with an impenetrable concrete slab above. Viewed through the lens of the glass ceiling metaphor, the building takes on a darker reading that echoes some truths about barriers that block paths to dreams.

Glass Ceilings in Fairy Tales

The image of women sealed inside of glass containers persists in Western fairy tales. In these stories, metaphoric use of reflective and luminous materials, including glass, reveals alternative readings of glass ceilings. Words like *beauty* and *golden* make recurring appearances in fairy tales. According to Max Lüthi, a Swiss literary theorist, gold stands for the highest expression of beauty.[57] Princesses in Grimm's tales have gold on their hairs and fingers and are surrounded by golden cups, chairs, and household objects. While not as prevalent as gold, glass and crystal also appear in these tales, "with its striving towards the clear, the unambiguous, the extreme, and the distinct."[58] Glass is often a metaphor of transformation in people, perhaps because the process of making glass is a transformation of an ordinary material – sand – into an extraordinarily delicate, crystalline material.[59] In the story of Cinderella, the glass slipper she loses at midnight comes to symbolize exquisite beauty, transforming a maid into an object of pursuit. Glass appears in the forms of slippers, mountains, and coffins and, as Lüthi observes, they are "breakable yet seldom broken."[60]

Seen in this light, glass in fairy tales offers renewed insights into the 2016 election night. In a 20th-century crystal palace in Manhattan, the public was held in suspense as Hillary Clinton anticipated celebrating her dream – to become the first female president of the United States. In fairy tales, beauty may be attributed to both male and female figures. However, with male figures a beautiful, or handsome, appearance is a characteristic that often accompanies their heroic actions. Conversely, physical beauty is the central focus in heroines.[61] With Clinton, the audience at the Javits Center celebrated Clinton's heroic actions to run for candidacy and to reach near-victory. In the conventions of traditional fairy tales, her action is celebrated as if she is a male hero.

Glass in fairy tales is also associated with the preservation of beauty and youth. It stands for an appearance of fragility, but is rarely shown broken, and it preserves its otherwise decaying contents in an unspoiled, pure state. In the Brothers Grimm's tales *Glass Coffin* and *Snow White*, the seven dwarves place the maiden in a glass casket after she eats a poisoned apple and dies. The dwarves look into the casket that is transparent on all visible sides and say, "although we cannot wake her, we must watch her well and keep her safe from harm."[62] Under the dwarves' careful guard, she remains preserved for years without deterioration. One day, a prince passes by and discovers the casket. He is taken by her beauty and asks the dwarves for the maiden. While carrying the casket to the castle, the servants stumble over a tree stump, which causes the poisoned apple in her throat to become dislodged. She awakens, and then the prince asks her to marry him (Figure 4.12).

FIGURE 4.12 The prince awakes Snow White sleeping in a glass coffin. Franz Jüttner (1865–1925).

Illustration from *Sneewittchen*, Scholz' Künstler-Bilderbücher, Mainz, 1905.

In the story, the female body is exhibited to observers to be discovered and rescued from outside the case. The glass is not broken from within. Snow White is seen as a beautiful, passive object, never deteriorating for the years following her apparent death while sealed in glass. The association of glass with the preservation of beauty assists this story. In museums, the most precious artifacts are placed under a glass case, exposed to the gaze of observers and artificially protected from deterioration and aging. Similarly, Cinderella's glass slipper transparently revealed her true beauty, as distinguished from her low status as a scullery maid. Isobel Armstrong, a scholar on Victorian glass culture, observes, "Glass became the founding element of the story – it was essential that the glass slipper fitted the right person – and Cinderella's magical transformation became mediated by glass."[63] Similarly today, glass mediates the dismantling of the barrier to women's advancement and their transition to positions of power.

Clear Glass Not Clear of Obstructions

The glass ceiling is "an unacknowledged barrier to advancement in a profession, especially affecting women and members of minorities."[64] Clear glass is not clear of obstructions. While the technical advancement of glass enables wider uses and more choices for architects and clients, high-tech glass increasingly contradicts the supposed intangible property of glass. Paper-thin, chemically strengthened glass, for one, exemplifies the dangerous subtlety of a thin, but unbreakable and tangible, barrier.

John Ruskin, a critic of the Crystal Palace wrote, "You can never have noble architecture in transparent or lustrous glass."[65] To Ruskin, a building not built with actions of the human hand, namely masonry, is less than noble. He was dismissive of a skeletal building, assembled from machine-produced parts, that appears to dissolve into the sky. Conversely, the German critic Lothar Buchner applauded the boundless, blurred edge between building and sky, writing that the Crystal Palace "dissolves into a distant background where all materiality is blended into the atmosphere,"[66] The Javits Center, like its precedent, appears to dissolve into the sky, through its gossamer skeletal structure when seen from the interior, and through its glass reflecting the sky when viewed from the outside.

Despite its diaphanous appearance, the glass is shatter-resistant. Following the presidential election of 2016 (Figure 4.13), the sky beyond the glass ceiling remains elusive. Marilyn Loden hoped for a day when yearning for the broken

FIGURE 4.13 John Podesta, campaign chairman, announces that Democratic presidential nominee Hillary Clinton will not be making an appearance at the Jacob Javits Center in New York, Wednesday, November 9, 2016 as the votes are still being counted.

Photograph: Jonathan Newton/ *The Washington Post.*

ceiling would be a fairy tale of the past – a time when the glass ceiling's enchant-ment was broken, the suspense was over, and women triumphed. Over 40 years after she coined the phrase, however, Loden fears it may outlive her.[67]

Notes

1 "Hillary Clinton: We Just Put the Biggest Crack in That Glass Ceiling," *Bloomberg*, July 26, 2016, accessed March 2, 2017, www.bloomberg.com/politics/videos/2016-07-27/hillary-clinton-we-just-put-the-biggest-crack-in-glass-ceiling.
2 Isobel Armstrong, *Victorian Glassworlds: Glass Culture and the Imagination 1830–1880* (Oxford: Oxford University Press, 2008), 175.
3 Armstrong, *Victorian Glassworlds*, 167.
4 Sharon Bernstein, "Highest Glass Ceiling Remains Intact after Clinton's Stunning Loss," *Reuters*, November 9, 2017, accessed March 4, 2017, www.reuters.com/article/us-usa-election-women-idUSKBN1341Q0
5 Amy Spiro, "Hillary Clinton and the Glass Ceiling: Cracked but Intact," *Jerusalem Post*, November 9, 2017, accessed March 4, 2017, www.jpost.com/Us-Election-Results/Hillary-Clinton/Hillary-Clinton-and-the-glass-ceiling-cracked-but-intact-472,112
6 Rosemarie Haag Bletter, "The Interpretation of the Glass-Dream Expressionist Architecture and the History of the Crystal Metaphor," *Journal of the Society of Architectural Historians* 40, no. 1 (March, 1981), 20–43.
7 Carol Hymowitz and Timothy D. Schellhardt, "The Glass Ceiling: Why Women Can't Seem to Break the Invisible Barrier that Blocks them from the Top Jobs," *The Wall Street Journal*, March 24, 1986, 61.
8 Marjorie Stockford, *The Bellwomen: The Story of the Landmark AT&T Sex Discrimination Case* (New Brunswick, NJ: Rutgers University Press, 2004). In 1878, Alexander Graham Bell replaced rude teenage boy operators with women who were politer and had pleasant voices.
9 Marilyn Loden, "Revisiting the Glass Ceiling," Loden Associates, Inc., accessed April 20, 2017, www.loden.com/Site/Site/Articles%20-%20Videos%20-%20Survey/C615CFE8-A70C-4E3A-9F81-8EACB0E087D0.html
10 Loden, "Revisiting the Glass Ceiling."
11 Marilyn Loden, *Feminine Leadership, or How to Succeed in Business Without Being One of the Boys* (New York: Crown, 1985).
12 Loden, "Revisiting the Glass Ceiling."
13 Rebecca Shambaugh, *It's Not a Glass Ceiling, It's a Sticky Floor: Free Yourself from the Hidden Behaviors Sabotaging Your Career Success* (New York: McGraw Hill, 2007).
14 Shambaugh *It's Not a Glass Ceiling.*
15 Ben Zimmer, "The Phrase 'Glass Ceiling' Stretches Back Decades; A Possible Start: A Conversation between Two Women in 1979," *The Wall Street Journal*, April 3, 2015, accessed March 4, 2017, www.wsj.com/articles/the-phrase-glass-ceiling-stretches-back-decades-1,428,089,010.
16 Glass Ceiling Commission, accessed April 29, 2017, http://nationalglassceilingcommission.org.
17 Hymowitz and Schellhardt, "The Glass Ceiling," 61.
18 Hymowitz and Schellhardt, "The Glass Ceiling," 61.
19 Zoe Williams, "The Glass Ceiling: A Metaphor that Needs to be Smashed," *The Guardian*, July 27, 2016, accessed April 16, 2017 www.theguardian.com/us-news/2016/jul/27/hillary-clinton-glass-ceiling-metaphor-that-needs-to-be-smashed
20 Williams, "The Glass Ceiling."
21 Marilyn Loden, phone interview by author, June 25, 2018.

22 Gottfried Semper, *Style in the Technical and Tectonic Arts, or Practical Aesthetics*, trans. Harry Francis Mallgrave (Los Angeles, CA: Getty, 2004), 147.

23 Semper, *Style in the Technical and Tectonic Arts*, 147.

24 Paul Scheerbart and Bruno Taut, *Glass Architecture and Alpine Architecture*, ed. Dennis Sharp; *Glass Architecture* trans. James Palmes; *Alpine Architecture* trans. Shirley Palmer New York: Praeger, 1972), 41.

25 Bletter, "The Interpretation of the Glass-Dream," 21.

26 Annette Fierro, *The Glass State: The Technology of the Spectacle, Paris, 1981–1998* (Cambridge, MA: MIT Press, 2003), 171. In this book, Fierro writes extensively on the glass transparency of the *Grand Projets* commissioned by the government of France under François Mitterand.

27 Fierro, *The Glass State*, 171.

28 Deborah Ascher Barnstone, *The Transparent State: Architecture and Politics in Postwar Germany* (Abingdon: Routledge, 2005), 175–208. Barnstone argues that despite the architect's use of glass to symbolize an open, accessible, and democratic parliament, there is little transparency in the stone Reichstag. Instead, Foster's design is transparent in the way in which it reveals German history through the building, including the graffiti, which Foster fought to preserve.

29 Perry Chin, project architect of the Javits Center at I. M. Pei and Partners, phone interview by author, April 13, 2017.

30 Deborah Dietsch, "Space Frame Odyssey: Jacob K. Javits Convention Center, New York City," *Architectural Record* 174, no. 10 (1986), 108.

31 Mitchell B. Rouda, "Dazzling Problems Plagued 'Crystal Palace': Manhattan's Javits Center, I. M. Pei & Partners," *Architecture* 76, no. 3 (1987), 95.

32 "Crystal Palace à New York: Jacob K. Javits Convention Center, New York City, I. M. Pei and Partners," *L'Architecture d'Aujourd'hui* 248, no. 12 (1986), XLIV.

33 Julie Iovine, "Slick but Classy: New York City's Convention Center: A New Romantism," *Connoisseur* 7 (July, 1986), 39.

34 Aaron Seward, "Javits Convention Center Renovation," *Architects Newspaper*, June 20, 2011, accessed August 30, 2019. https://archpaper.com/2011/06/javits-convention-center-renovation/

35 "Crystal Palace à New York," XLIV.

36 Chin, phone interview.

37 *Merriam-Webster, s.v.* "ceiling," accessed April 13, 2017, www.merriam-webster.com/dictionary/ceiling.

38 Rem Koolhaas et al., *Elements of Architecture: 14* (Venice: Biennale di Venezia, 2014, back cover).

39 Kenneth Frampton and Yukio Futagawa, *Modern Architecture 1851–1945* (Milan: Rizzoli, 1983).

40 Ralph Lieberman, "Crystal Palace, a Late Twentieth Century View of its Changing Place in Architectural History and Criticism," *AA Files* 12 (Summer, 1986), 46–58.

41 John McKean, *Crystal Palace* (London: Phaidon, 1994), 14.

42 Armstrong, *Victorian Glassworlds*, 170.

43 Armstrong, *Victorian Glassworlds*, 175.

44 Armstrong, *Victorian Glassworlds*, 169.

45 *Notice of Acceptance #10-0413.04 issued to E.I. Dupont De Nemours & Co. Inc.* (Miami: Miami-Dade County Building Code Compliance Office, 2010). Ionoplast interlayer is elaborated in this book's chapter on the Apple Store's 5th Avenue glass cube.

46 *Trosifol Architectural Laminated Glass Interlayers: Product Portfolio for Laminators* (Wilmington: Kuraray Group, 2016).

47 "Corning® Gorilla® Glass Technology Overview," Corning Inc., accessed March 4, 2017, www.corning.com/gorillaglass/worldwide/en/technology/technology-overview.html.

48 "Corning® Gorilla® Glass Technology Overview."

49 "Gorilla® Glass: Why Glass Breaks," Corning, Inc., accessed March 4, 2017, www. corning.com/gorillaglass/worldwide/en/videos/why-glass-breaks.html.

50 Wolfgang Schivelbusch, "Policing of Street Lighting," *Yale French Studies, 73, Everyday Life* (1987), 62–65.

51 Glass Ceiling Commission, accessed April 29, 2017, http://nationalglassceilingcom mission.org/.

52 Koolhaas et al., *Elements of Architecture: 14,*152.

53 Rouda, "Dazzling Problems Plagued 'Crystal Palace,'"100.

54 German structural engineering firm Schlaich Bergermann Partner (SBP) was a pioneer in designing cable net glass walls, beginning with the 1993 Kempinski Hotel façade in Munich. Over the past two decades, this façade type has become more widely built, including the Time Warner Center and the Alice Tully Hall in New York City.

55 Joe Welker, SOM project architect for the Time Warner Center, email message to author, April 16, 2017.

56 Lisa W. Foderaro, "Renovation at Javits Center Alleviates Hazard for Manhattan's Birds," *New York Times*, September 4, 2015, accessed April 16, 2017, www. nytimes.com/2015/09/05/nyregion/making-the-javits-center-less-deadly-for-birds. html?_r=0.

57 Max Lüthi, *The Fairytale as Art Form and Portrait of Man* (Bloomington, IN: Indiana UP, 1987), 15.

58 Lüthi, *The Fairytale as Art Form*, 15.

59 Carina Hart, "Glass Beauty: Coffins and Corpses in A.S. Byatt's *Possession*," *Marvels & Tales* 26, no. 2 (2012), 205.

60 Lüthi, *The Fairytale as Art Form*, 15.

61 Lüthi, *The Fairytale as Art Form*, 13.

62 The Brothers Grimm, *Snow White and the Seven Dwarfs*, trans. Wanda Gág (New York: Coward-McCann, 1938), 37.

63 Armstrong, *Victorian Glassworlds*, 205.

64 *Oxford Dictionary of English*, *s.v.* "glass ceiling," accessed August 7, 2019, www. lexico.com/en/definition/glass_ceiling.

65 John Ruskin, *Stones of Venice: The Foundations* (Sunnyside, UK: George Allen, 1886), 380.

66 Lothar Buchner quoted in Lieberman, "Crystal Palace," 56.

67 Theresa Vargas, "She Coined the Term 'Glass Ceiling.' She Fears it Will Outlive her," *Washington Post*, March 1, 2018, accessed July 30, 2018, www.washington post.com/news/retropolis/wp/2018/03/01/she-coined-the-phrase-glass-ceiling-she-didnt-expect-it-to-outlive-her/?utm_term=.51f07e6fcecc

5

AIR, LIGHT, AND LIQUID IN MOTION
The Glass Pavilion in Toledo

The Glass Pavilion at the Toledo Museum of Art (Figure 5.1), designed by Kazuyo Sejima and Ryue Nishizawa of SANAA, presents a novel kind of transparency that results from layering of clear glass and volumes of air. Built with clear glass as the primary exterior walls and interior partitions, the Pavilion is simultaneously both opaque and transparent in its construction and spatial organization. It is opaque in its concealment of steel structure which makes the transparent ribbons of massive glass possible. At the same time, it is remarkably transparent in exposing elements of architecture that are typically hidden from view, notably the plenum made of clear glass. These see-through plenums make radical programmatic adjacencies and visual connections. These novel transparencies result from several mutually dependent factors: an innovative approach to mechanical and structural engineering, balance of light, reversal of structural and material hierarchies, and a novel spatial organization of glass-enclosed air plenums and rooms to create a complex array of reflections. This unusual organization of air and glass can be traced to human breath that, prior to industrialization, shaped molten glass into blown cylinders, which were then cut and flattened into thin sheets. The exhalation of air from human lungs transformed molten glass into a frozen liquid. Isobel Armstrong, a scholar in British literary and cultural studies, writes that glass bequeathed the "congealed residue of someone else's breath … annealed in the substance he worked."[1] The Glass Pavilion's transparency is soft, watery, and intimately airy – in contrast to the hard, cold, machine-made impression often associated with glass (Figure 5.2).

The softness of the Pavilion is further underscored by its play of layered reflections. The Glass Pavilion is a carefully calibrated instrument of light, shadow, and reflection. Although clear glass is the predominant material, the building differs from the see-through transparency of modernism described as

FIGURE 5.1 Each space of the Pavilion is enclosed by a curved, transparent low-iron glass wall. An open-air courtyard (left) is seen next to a glass-enclosed interior gallery (right).

Photograph: Iwan Baan (2007).

FIGURE 5.2 Layered reflections seen through the double-glazed buffer zone for air. The Glass Pavilion's transparency is soft, watery, and intimately airy.

Photograph: Iwan Baan (2007).

shadowless glass box in Ludwig Hilberseimer's 1929 essay *Glasarchitektur*. He writes that the Crystal Palace built in 1850 to 1851 "obliterated the old opposition of light and shadow, which had formed the properties of past architecture. It made a space of evenly distributed brightness; it created a room of shadowless light."[2] Likewise, the Pavilion is distinguished from the diffused, shadowy luminosity of translucent glass buildings. In contrast, the use of curved, massive monolithic glass in the Pavilion leads to an intensified transparency in which a clear material gives mutable readings ranging from apparent depth to near-opacity. This layering of glass and air engenders a glass transparency of deep, dense, yet diaphanous space that differs from ordinary curtain wall skyscrapers, or the canonical modern glass buildings such as the Farnsworth House. Reflections seen through multiple curved glass sheets belie the material's characterization as merely transparent.

A Glass Building Made for Glass

The original Toledo Museum of Art was founded in 1901 by the owners of Libbey-Owens Sheet Glass Company,[3] a maker of windshields for the automobile industry and sheet glass for building construction. The Glass Pavilion completed in 2006 is a freestanding, one-story museum that exhibits a collection of over 7,000 glass objects (Figure 5.3) and production processes. It stands across

FIGURE 5.3 A collection of over 7,000 glass objects are exhibited in bubble-like glass rooms.

Photograph: Author (2012).

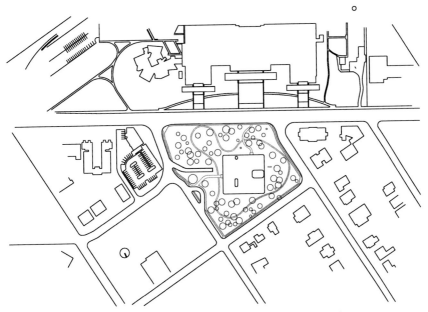

FIGURE 5.4 Site plan showing the Glass Pavilion in a park across the street from the main museum built in 1901, and the Frank Gehry addition built in 1992 to the south. SANAA (2006).

the street from the main museum, on a flat site among 150-year-old trees.[4] (Figures 5.4 and 5.5) The name Pavilion was chosen by the Museum to imply a separate structure in a garden, such as a tent, that is built for pleasure. The Glass Pavilion is a place of sensory pleasure; 4,000 years of glass history is seen in and through layers of bubble-shaped glass enclosures that flow into each other like liquid.

Glass Layered with Air

Each individual room in the Pavilion is enclosed by a curving wall of low-iron, monolithic laminated glass panels three-quarters of an inch thick. "Our concept is to wrap each program [element] with a curved line drawn by a single stroke of [the] brush," writes SANAA's principal Ryue Nishizawa.[5] The program elements include exhibition rooms for glass crafts, multipurpose rooms, open-air courtyards, storage, and hot glass demonstration shops. In order to keep the main floor free of visual obstructions as much as possible, the mechanical rooms are located in the basement, and the cooling towers and pumps are off-site in a separate building.[6] Heating pipes and cooling ducts are located in the floor of the Pavilion to prevent condensation and provide thermal comfort (Figure 5.6).[7] On the main floor,

FIGURE 5.5 The Pavilion stands across the street from the main museum, on a flat site among 150-year-old trees.

Photograph: Nicholas Coates (2013).

FIGURE 5.6 Heating pipes and cooling ducts are located below the Pavilion floor, accessible from the basement.

Photograph: Nicholas Coates (2013).

FIGURE 5.7 Bubble-like interior glass rooms create a 30-inch air cavity in between spaces.

Photograph: Nicholas Coates (2013).

FIGURE 5.8 In between bubble-like interior glass rooms and the exterior glass wall is a 30-inch buffer zone of air.

Photograph: Nicholas Coates (2013).

enclosing all bubble-like rooms is an exterior envelope of the same glass but at a greater thickness of one inch. Interior glass rooms float within the exterior envelope's continuous glass skin, separated from each other by a 30-inch air cavity (Figures 5.7, 5.8, and 5.9). This zone of air mitigates temperature differences between the outdoor and the conditioned indoor spaces, as well as between the galleries and the shops with glass kilns. It is unlike the air cavity found in standard double-glass façades, or the mechanical shafts and spaces concealed in opaque stud walls. This transparent cavity flows like water through the building to make a contiguous air cushion. It expands and contracts as it turns rounded corners but maintains a minimum egress clearance for people to pass through for maintenance – a hallway for air. This perimeter air zone closely resembles Taut's writing in his 1913 book *Alpine Architecture*. He describes the Crystal House in one of his drawings, "Building material is of Glass only. Between the glass shell of the interior and the outer glass shell of the house is a large space, which serves for heating and ventilation."[8] Taut had recognized the challenge of heating and cooling an all-glass building and anticipated a solution in double-glazing.

This soft, sensual layering of curved glass and air is a reminder of the former liquid state of molten glass, molded by the exhalation of air from human lungs and transformed into a solid. This infusion of matter with spirit is marked in the process of heroic glassmaking by human bodies. Armstrong writes, "Held up to the light a piece of common nineteenth-century glass will display small

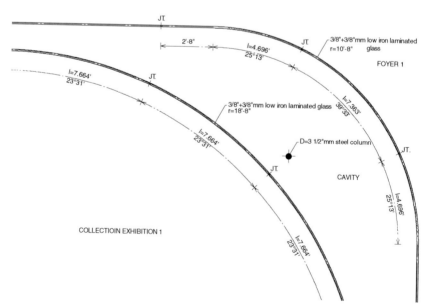

FIGURE 5.9 Plan of interstitial airspace, a hallway for air, at the building perimeter. SANAA (2006).

blemishes, blisters, almost invisible striae, spectral undulations that are the marks of bodily labour and a brief expectation of life."[9]

The visual effect that results from this glass-wrapped air cavity is that of reflection and re-reflection of objects and people in motion layered upon each other, creating a mutable palimpsest of images (Figure 5.10). Like the Hall of Mirrors in Versailles, but with a greater subtlety, the Toledo Pavilion presents a theatricality of seeing oneself seeing. Annette Fierro draws comparison between the glass reflections at Fondation Cartier and those in Dan Graham's work: "The overlay is often complexly orchestrated to multiply and distort the position of the viewer and the viewed against an unfolding space of reflected landscape."[10] Whereas Graham's glass sheets have metallic coating intended to reflect the surrounding environment, SANAA decidedly specified uncoated glass[11]. Consequently, the reflections are less obvious. From some angles, the layers of transparent glass

FIGURE 5.10 Reflections and re-reflections of objects and people in motion are layered upon each other, creating a mutable palimpsest of mobile images.

Photograph: Nicholas Coates (2013).

appear to create a density of near-opaque material, whereas from perspectives, one can see through the entire building to the Victorian houses and trees beyond.

Each of the 360 glass panels, measuring thirteen-and-a-half feet tall and weighing 1,300 to 1,500 pounds,[12] were manufactured in Pilkington's factory in Germany. They were shipped to Shenzhen, China where they were slumped (a process of shaping glass panels over mold at high temperature) and laminated with polyvinyl butyral (PVB) interlayer to fabricate the thick mono-lithic panels (Figure 5.11).[13] Visible materials and structures other than glass are made inconspicuous. Slender steel columns of three-and-a-half inch to four-and-a-quarter inch diameter support spans as long as 60 feet and hold up a shallow roof of two-feet deep.[14] The bottom of the glass wall panels rest on recessed tracks in the concrete floor, and are held in place laterally by another track concealed in the ceiling.[15] The roof is designed to float over the glass and never bear on the glass panels.[16] Neither SANAA nor the client intended their transparent building to carry an ideological message. The choice of glass as a material stems from its industrial ties to Toledo, a former glassmaking capital of the country for automobiles, building products, and houseware. Furthermore, the Pavilion does not use glass to exhibit the technological

FIGURE 5.11 Glass panel being tilted in place on site. Curved steel tracks for glass are exposed below the roof until the ceiling conceals them.

Photograph: Front inc. (2006).

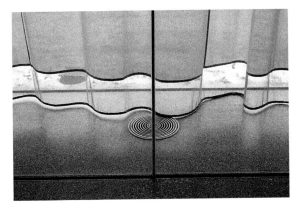

FIGURE 5.12 Two sheets of glass are held together at the vertical joint with translucent structural silicone. Circular air grill and sheer curtains are located in the perimeter air zone between the interior glass partition and the exterior glass wall.

Photograph: Nicholas Coates (2013).

spectacle of the structure as, for example, the Pompidou and the Louvre Pyramid showcase customized steel connections. Instead, SANAA strategically conceals the structure in tightly concentrated opaque gypsum walls and ceilings, and any visible columns are made as inconspicuous as possible.

Where two sheets of glass meet at a vertical joint, they are held with translucent structural silicone. In this way, there are no vertical mullions or channels (Figure 5.12). Since the glass panels are monolithic and not insulated glass units (IGUs), the building has no desiccant-holding metal spacers that become visible vertical joints in IGUs. The result is that the Pavilion glass walls appear continuous and ribbon-like.[17] In the Toledo Pavilion, the layering of multiple glass-enclosed spaces and the organization of the rooms alongside day-lit courtyards are deliberate design moves that result in curious spatial effects. The glass appears neither opaque nor completely transparent. It does not simply allow the interior and exterior to be seen simultaneously; it presents layered reflections of the nearby trees, cars, and houses, overlapping them with the objects and world beyond and before the glass walls (Figure 5.13).

Glass Translucency and Opacity

Complexity achieved with translucent rather than transparent glass is found in early modern and recent examples. The exterior diamond-shaped dome of Bruno Taut's Glass Pavilion in Cologne (1914) consisted of two layers of glass (Figure 5.14). The outer layer of plate glass was framed by concrete ribs. The inner layer was made up of 4-inch x 4-inch prismatic tiles held together by eletroglazing,[18] a process by which glass tiles were joined using copper strips

FIGURE 5.13 Layered reflections of the nearby trees, cars, and houses, overlapping with the objects and world beyond the glass walls.

Photograph: Nicholas Coates (2013).

and an electrolytic bath to make rigid window panels watertight.[19] Placed between two glass block walls was the staircase consisting of steel frames filled with prismatic glass tiles.[20] The light inside the stairway surrounded by prismatic glass bounced across the space and back, exponentially multiplying the effect of illumination.

Maison de Verre (1932) by Pierre Chareau (Figure 5.15) projects the shadowy presence of its occupants onto the translucent glass block façade. In order to provide privacy for the doctor's family and patients while illuminating the interior, the steel frame façades are infilled with Saint Gobain's 20cm x 20cm x 4cm Nevada-type glass lenses that diffuse light with their concave section profile and textured patterns.[21] The appearance is remarkably like the translucency of skin when light passes behind it. After World War II, mirrored glass façades came to symbolize corporate architecture such as Eero Saarinen's

FIGURE 5.14 Bruno Taut's Glass Pavilion in Cologne (1914). Stairs are located between two sheets of glass block walls.

Photograph: Canadian Centre for Architecture.

laboratories for IBM and Bell Telephone (1961 and 1966). As Reinhold Martin argues, these vast façades reflected the corporation's organizational complex more than the landscape that surrounded it.[22]

In his book *The Architectural Uncanny* (1992), Anthony Vidler writes that transparency was gradually discredited over the 70s and the 80s.[23] During this period, the opacity of post-modern buildings dominated architectural discourse. Vidler further observes an "uncanny repetition"[24] of transparent glass building revival that followed post-modernism. France built Parisian *Grands Projets* as the symbol of political transparency. In the 1989 French national library competition entry by Rem Koolhaas, however, Vidler finds a different kind of glass sensibility. The glass cube, he discerns, "is conceived as a solid, not as a void, with interior volumes carved out of a crystalline block." Its "organs" – the interior rooms and circulation spaces – in "amoebic suspension," would cast shadows, distinguishing themselves from a shadowless modern glass box.[25]

FIGURE 5.15 Maison de Verre (1932) by Pierre Chareau projects the shadowy presence of its occupants onto the translucent glass block façade.

Photograph: Bianca Maggio.

In 1995, the Museum of Modern Art (MoMA) organized the exhibition *Light Construction*. In the opening paragraph of the accompanying exhibition catalog, curator Terence Riley remarks on the emergence of a new architectural sensibility that investigates the potential of architectural surfaces. This exhibition nearly aligned with an increased focus in the mid-1990s on material investigations both in practice and academia.[26] Riley suggests that the projects in the exhibition offer sensibilities that contrast the bright, shadowless light of glass buildings described by Ludwig Hilberseimer early in the 20th century.[27] Prevalent among the exhibited buildings are translucent acid-etched glass, perforated metal screens, alabaster that transmits light, and photographic images "tattooed" on marble surfaces. The exhibition showed how the use of these thin materials or surface treatments of materials could offer architects new vocabularies. The achieved effects, however, were primarily realized with either translucent or perforated opaque materials, not clear glass. In recent years, a host of buildings with multi-layered, *shoji* screen-like translucent glass has been built, exemplified by Zumthor's Kunsthaus Bregenz (1997) (Figure 5.16) and Steven Holl's Nelson-Atkins Museum of Art (2008). At Kunsthaus

FIGURE 5.16   Light from the translucent glass ceiling filters light into the gallery at Kunsthaus Bregenz (1997) by Peter Zumthor.

Photograph: Author (2018).

Bregenz, sunlight is filtered through multiple acid-etched glass sheets, first in the vertical walls then the horizontal ceilings, to make galleries glow softly in indirect but changing natural light. At The Nelson-Atkins Museum, capillary glass tubes are sandwiched between channel glass, delicately scattering rays of light in multiple directions. The effect is that of luminous glaciers sliding across the landscape. Contrarily to the shadowless, see-through glass boxes, these examples amplify the effects of shadows on translucent glass.

What distinguishes the transparency at SANAA's Glass Pavilion from that of modern glass boxes, postwar mirrored office buildings, or contemporary translucent structures? The Glass Pavilion is exceptional in its use of crystal clear glass to achieve qualities infrequently found in a transparent material alone. The architects' approach to thermal and structural engineering, structure-partition hierarchy, spatial organization, and lighting are made mutually dependent upon each other to bring to life a new kind of transparency.

Glass Transparency and Thermal Cushion

The effect of extraordinary transparency at SANAA's Glass Pavilion is intrinsically related to the problem of heating and cooling and, subsequently, the architects' integration of engineering with architecture. Questions of heating and cooling glass buildings challenged modern architects from their early days. Bruno Taut's Glass Pavilion in Cologne and Paul Scheerbart's book *Glasarchitektur*, both dated 1914, foreshadowed a future in glass buildings with double-glazed walls, including their capacity to solve glass's critical weakness, thermal transfer. Like Taut, Scheerbart believed that technology was "the formative agent of the current culture"[28] and saw the need to experiment with glass architecture enabled by iron structure. Taut invited Scheerbart to write 14 mottos in rhyming couplets in German, each in 28 letters. These words were incised around the concrete at the base of the dome. One of the 14 phrases by Scheerbart explicitly referenced a double glass wall: "Greater than the diamond is the double walled glass house."[29] Scheerbart speculated that interaction between two sheets of glass held a greater potential than a single lite, anticipating the transparent *poché* space between the curved sheets of glass at Toledo. In Scheerbart's prophetic 1914 book *Glasarchitektur*, he contemplated double glass, looking far ahead of his time to speculate what glass architecture could be. He wrote, "As air is one of the worst conductors of heat, the double glass wall is an essential condition for all glass architecture. The walls can be a meter apart – or have an even greater space between."[30]

What is remarkable is not only the dimensional similarity between the perimeter air circulation zone at SANAA's building in Toledo and what Scheerbart describes as glass walls "a meter apart." It is also that the "light between these walls shine outward and inward."[31] The play of light between the layered sheets of glass at Toledo makes the reflections and their refraction appear superimposed on each other, constructing a delicate, diaphanous space, and suggesting a new sort of transparency. Moreover, Scheerbart forecast double glazing as a response to the problem of heat conduction with glass. What Taut and Scheerbart envisioned with two sheets of glass spaced about a meter apart bears a notable resemblance to the 30-inch air space at the Toledo Glass Pavilion.

There were other modern architects who notably pioneered environmental control in glass façade buildings. Early examples of double glass façades first appeared in industrial buildings, including the Steiff factory in Giengen, Germany (1903) and Olivetti's ICO factory in Ivrea, Italy by Figini and Pollini (1937–1939). These buildings were designed for laborers who worked by natural daylight and ventilation. In the late 1920s, Le Corbusier gave the name "neutralizing wall" to the double skin façade that cuts heat transfer between the inside and the outside and, instead, circulates mechanically conditioned air in the cavity. He proposed the neutralizing wall for the League of Nations assembly hall in Geneva (1927), the Tsentrosoyuz office building in Moscow (1929–1935), and the Salvation Army City of Refuge in Paris (1930–33). The double façade was only implemented at the Tsentrosoyuz building, but with operable windows. The City of Refuge was built with a non-operable airtight glass façade, but was only single-glazed.[32]

Engineering Glass Transparency

Since the energy crises of the early 1970s, the pressure for buildings to perform thermally has become a political and economic matter. Despite well-publicized poor thermal performance of some LEED (Leadership in Energy and Environmental

Design)-certified buildings and the notion of "greenwashing,"[33] there is an undeniable influence by programs such as LEED on the types of materials that architects specify. Yet, excessive use of frits, tints, reflective coating, and sunshades to manage solar gain are counter to achieving the transparency that made glass the choice material in the first place. Unlike recent glass buildings with a chemical coating or other property-altering materials applied to the glass, the Toledo Glass Pavilion relies on low-iron glass laminated with clear interlayer, which by itself is relatively conventional. The effects are achieved not with a chemical coating or application of other materials but with the spatial organization of crystal clear glass bubble-like rooms placed within a larger glass bubble. Careful considerations for light balance and engineering allow the behaviors of light on glass to surface to the foreground.

The Glass Pavilion took an exceptionally integrative approach to climate control in a nearly all-glass building, a type that is notoriously difficult to cool and heat efficiently. SANAA worked with Transsolar, a climate engineering firm founded in Stuttgart, Germany.[34] Transsolar's climate control strategies contributed significantly to a different kind of material transparency. The Pavilion consists of three energy zones: the perimeter buffer zone, the hot glass demonstration areas, and the galleries with individual climate control requirements (Figure 5.17). The innovation in climate engineering lies in the perimeter zone and the mediation of thermal controls between the areas with variable climatic needs. The air in the first zone is tempered by hydronic radiant heating and cooling in the floor and ceiling. This moderates the difference in temperatures between the indoor and outdoor glass surfaces, which in turn prevents condensation on the glass in both hot and cold weathers. The Glass Pavilion takes additional innovative approaches to heating and cooling. The hot air generated in the hot glass demonstration spaces is recovered and redirected through a hydronic floor slab in order to heat other spaces in the building. Cool air collected from the galleries is used to cool the hot glass demonstration zones.[35] Na Min Mike Ra of Front, the glass consultants on this building, notes that recirculating the heat from the hot shop furnace, which is kept on 24/7, made an all-glass building possible in the cold climate of Toledo. Otherwise, the heating cost would have been prohibitively expensive.[36]

In SANAA's process, engineering is treated with as equal importance as other aspects of the design. Technical matters, including the details that guide the construction process and the placement of columns relative to the glass, are treated as integral aspects of visual appearance.[37] The means for heating, cooling, and ventilation are repressed into invisible locations beneath the floor or in a separate building to give the Pavilion a simple appearance, despite its highly complex mechanical systems. The Pavilion performs as an efficient, transparent organism, or what SANAA's project architect Toshihiro Oki calls, "a cohesive unit of systems."[38] At Toledo, SANAA's longtime collaborator Sasaki and Partners/SAP of Tokyo worked with the US engineering firm Guy Nordensen and Associates. The girders and joints, ductwork, and plumbing pipes reside within the two-foot

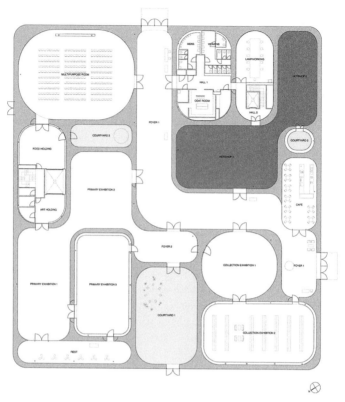

FIGURE 5.17 Plan color coded to indicate three energy zones: perimeter buffer zone (light gray), hot glass demonstration area (dark gray), and galleries with individual climate control requirements (white).

Plan courtesy of SANAA, with color coding by author (2006).

depth of the roof. Vertical runs for the pipes and ducts are housed in the full-height opaque walls. As with many of SANAA's buildings, such as the Naoshima Ferry Terminal (2006), with ultraslender columns, these opaque walls must also accommodate lateral bracing. The slender columns are mostly solid steel, but some are hollow to run infrastructure and rainwater between the roof and floor.[39] While both Mies and Johnson used opaque walls to house vertical infrastructure within otherwise all-glass wall buildings, the Toledo Pavilion is unique in its use of glass to build plenums. Whereas the occupants of both Mies and Johnson's glass houses viewed out to the landscape through a single layer of glass, at Toledo, the views become blurred through multiple layers of curved glass.

SANAA's buildings are a feat of mechanical and structural engineering. They appear deceptively simple and atectonic by comparison to the structural expressions of Peter Rice, Jörg Schlaich, or Norman Foster. In SANAA's work, the visible structure is minimized so that the atmospheric effects become foregrounded. In their essay "Ocean of Air," Cristina Diaz Moreno and Efren Garcia Grinda describe this phenomenon as "intensified perception in which the process of minimizing the object's main features (form, materials, size) takes priority over those usually regarded as secondary."[40]

Annette Fierro writes that the Barcelona Pavilion is a "transparent building rendered translucent by lack of honesty in the construction."[41] In this sense, the Toledo Glass Pavilion is both opaque and transparent – or "blurred." It is opaque in how it conceals its lateral bracing inside gypsum walls and its long-span steel beams inside the roof. The engineering that frees the glass walls of obstructions is not made readily apparent. On the other hand, its treatment of the plenum is strikingly transparent – the air that normally circulates within an opaque *poché* flows between two sheets of crystal clear glass. There is no attempt to hide the plenum, leaving ordinary museum visitors unaware of looking into transparent "air ducts."

Blurring of Tectonic Hierarchies

Since the founding of SANAA or, perhaps more accurately, since their days of working for Toyo Ito, suppression of the structure that supports their diaphanous buildings has been central to their design explorations. Kenneth Frampton points out a similar suppression of the structural system in Johnson's Glass House (1949). He writes that the glass, the steel frames, and the roof are nearly flush with each other, such that, unlike Mies's Farnsworth House (1951) that has a deep overhang, there is no shadow cast on the skin of the building.[42] Even though the houses were completed less than two years apart, the differences in reflections may be partly attributed to the different manufacturing method for the glass specified in these houses. Johnson's Glass House was glazed with quarter-inch thick plate glass,[43] which would have been shaped by roller and then hand polished. The glass at Mies's Farnsworth House was quarter-inch float glass,[44] made by floating molten glass on top of molten tin, and not polished, and therefore slightly lower in reflectivity. However, the difference in external reflectance of 8% for plate and 10% for float glass is barely perceptible.[45] A more plausible reason for the perceptual difference between the glasses is the play of (or the lack of) shadow cast by the roof.

On both the Glass House and the Toledo Pavilion, this suppression of structure and the lack of shadow bring the eyes to the effects of transparency, reflection, and refraction on glass. Frampton calls Johnson's approach *scenographic*, whereas Mies's is always *tectonic*.[46] The effects of SANAA's approach at Toledo veers towards the former, although the Glass Pavilion invites motion, like a film, whereas Johnson's house is akin to a still photo. Like Johnson's Glass House (Figure 5.18), the roof of the Toledo Glass Pavilion affords no overhang (Figure 5.19), thereby eliminating shadows on the glass walls and intensifying the play of reflections on glass. In a 2000 interview regarding their Illinois Institute of Technology Campus Center competition entry, Sejima says,

FIGURE 5.18 Philip Johnson's Glass House, January 01, 1948. The glass, the steel frames, and the roof are nearly flush with each other, such that there is no shadow cast on the skin of the building. The blurred reflections of the landscape are seen on the glass surfaces, overlapped with the views beyond.

Photograph: Ralph Morse (1948). The LIFE Picture Collection.

> We wanted to study an idea of reducing the usual hierarchy between structure and partition, where the structure comes first and partitions are infill. So we tried to make the structure disappear and the (glass) partitions very thick and heavy.[47]

As Ákos Moravánszky observes, this is an alternative, anti-tectonic reading of buildings that contrasts the classical readings of buildings based on tectonic expressions.[48] This reversal – or blurring – of hierarchy is also found at Toledo.

At the Glass Pavilion, there is relatively little hierarchy in the glass specification throughout the building. Both interior and exterior walls are monolithic laminated glass, just a quarter-inch thickness difference. The gray concrete floor with mineral aggregates is uniform throughout, from the air cavity and the corridors, to the galleries.[49] There is, however, a clear hierarchy in the served spaces – the galleries, the hot glass labs, and the multipurpose rooms – versus the service space between the bubble-shaped rooms, and in the basement and the roof. In other words, the mechanical spaces in this pavilion are the most visible spaces that make up the façades of the building and, at the same time, the most concealed spaces buried in the basement and a remote

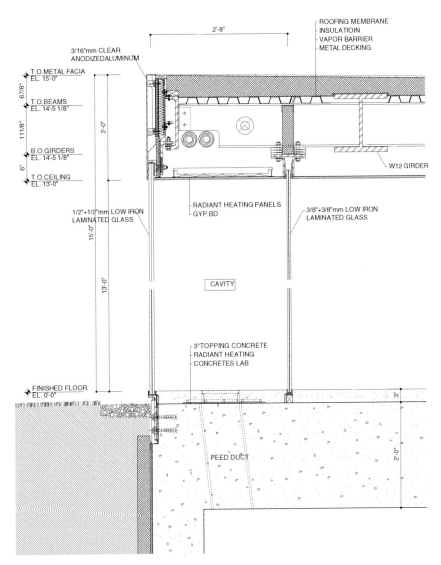

FIGURE 5.19 Section through perimeter plenum enclosed by floor-to-ceiling glass walls. The roof provides no overhang to shade the glass, which amplifies the effects of reflections on glass.

SANAA (2006).

building off-site.[50] Both the absence of hierarchy in glass and floor materials and the clear presence of service-served hierarchy bring about fluid transitions between spaces that vary considerably in performance and functions.

Glass Details and Plan Organization

At Toledo, SANAA took great care to make the glass construction details unobtrusive while amplifying their spatial effects. This was done through the treatment of seams, the specification of glass, edge finish, and the strategic placement of joints relative to the columns. Exposed glass edges in contemporary buildings are often highly polished to make them prismatic, then arrised (chamfered by a sixteenth of an inch). At Toledo, the edges at silicone joints were ground smooth but left unpolished[51] to draw the eye not to the material edges but to the effects on the expansive surfaces. Low-iron glass was specified to minimize the green tint of standard glass.[52] The architects finely tuned and calibrated the glass reflections. Even though they were interested in reflecting the site context on the glass walls, the effects differ from those of *Two-Way Mirror* by Dan Graham, for example. Oki recalled that they considered coating the glass to reduce reflections but not to increase them. Furthermore, reflective metal finishes are minimized in the building. The slender steel columns and light fixtures are finished in matte white. Exposed metals are limited to the stainless steel frames at the glass doors and the guardrails around exhibited objects, where the shine is reduced with a matte, directional brushed finish.[53] The occasional slender columns of only 3.5 or 4.25-inch diameter are purposely placed off the regular 8 foot x 8 foot grid so that the curved glass and its optical effects, not the column grid, take priority.[54]

The use of thick interior and exterior glass walls results in maximum transparency in a building type – a museum – that normally depends upon opaque walls to exhibit artifacts. The all-glass foyer physically separates, yet visually connects, the hot lab from the gallery; without this transparent thermal buffer, these two spaces with highly varied needs for temperature, moisture, and acoustics could not be next to each other unless separated by insulated opaque walls. From the glass-wrapped foyer between the gallery and the hot lab, a visitor can view glass sculptures and vessels against, in the background, the molten glass shaped into solid objects in the adjacent hot lab (Figure 5.20). Multiple states of glass appear simultaneously superimposed upon each other, through a plan organization enabled by a radical placement of thick monolithic glass. The superimposition is also temporal. Glass objects spanning a period of 4,000 year, from a Mesopotamian glass bowl to the Libbey Glass Company's punch bowls are viewed in a fluid transition from one enclosure to another.

Nishizawa's remark that they enclosed each program with a single brush stroke suggests a space different from one drawn with a pen. Similar to Western watercolor paintings, Japanese calligraphy and brush painting – *sumi-e* – achieve tonality by varying ink density with water. Less ink and more water

FIGURE 5.20 From the glass-wrapped foyer between the gallery and the hot lab, a visitor can view glass sculptures and vessels, against the molten glass shaped into solid objects in the adjacent hot lab.

Photograph: Nicholas Coates (2013).

are used for faint or distant scenes, and the strokes are layered to depict depth. Moreover, unlike a pen with uniform line width, a brush stroke varies in width and transparency depending on the pressure placed on the brush and the angle at which the brush glides across the paper. Like a brush stroke, the air cavity that surrounds each bubble-like enclosure in Toledo is contiguous and varies in width. Similar to multiple superimposed watery brush strokes with a faint hint of ink, transparent glass sheets suggest depth, and even opacity, when seen through multiple layers.

In 1996, Toyo Ito wrote an essay on his protégé Kazuyo Sejima's work, calling her "a new type of architect" and coined the phrase "Diagram Architecture" to characterize her work:

> If there is one way that best describes the spirit of her structures, it would be to say that it is "diagram architecture". In other words, that according to her, a building is ultimately the equivalent of the diagram of the space used to abstractly describe the mundane activities presupposed by the structure.[55]

The design process of the Toledo Glass Pavilion suggests that the design emerged out of a conversion of an adjacency or "bubble diagram" to a building. Oki remarks that the cavity wall was neither a stated goal nor the result of environmental design, but it came about in spatial studies of programmatic adjacencies. He explains that the bubble-shaped spaces were drawn to delineate programmatic proximities that the museum needed. Then, in working with mechanical and structural engineers, there emerged material and spatial relationships that the architects imagined would bear unusual atmospheric effects in transparent glass.[56] The transparency found in the Glass Pavilion is an exquisite materialization of Diagram Architecture, an adjacency diagram converted to crystal clear glass with brevity, as Ito characterized.

Balancing Light at Different Times of the Day

The specific optical effects of the building are presumably not what Sejima and Nishizawa started out by imagining. When speaking about their installation at the Barcelona Pavilion, they said, "We try not to select options for which we can already imagine the outcome." Beatriz Colomina calls this "an architecture of deliberately unclear vision."[57] On the one hand, Oki affirms this was the case in Toledo. On the other, the building is an exquisite lens carefully and deliberately calibrated for optical effects. He says,

> Glass has the ability to reflect the seasons, the colors, and the sky. That gives a different kind of atmosphere on any given day or season ... That possibility is what they (Sejima and Nishizawa) were interested in. But that's the unknown in a way ... You have an idea, but until you see it built, you don't know for sure.[58]

On the one hand, effects are unknown, but on the other, the Pavilion is marked by the precision and discipline characteristic of SANAA. The effects are not accidental.

Oki recalled in an interview,

> We talked a lot about the light level. Light level determined transparency and reflection of glass ... One extreme instance is night time. During the day when it's darker inside and brighter outside, everything is transparent [when looking out from the interior].[59]

The architects introduced ways to balance the light levels between inside and outside. At night time when electric light makes the interior brighter than the exterior, the vision of those inside the museum is dominated by the reflections of themselves and the interior objects. To counter this, the surrounding landscape is made artificially brighter to balance the light levels inside and out (Figure 5.21). This neutralizes the extreme differences and makes the glass

FIGURE 5.21 The landscape surrounding the Pavilion is artificially illuminated more brightly to balance the light levels inside and out. Here, the snow on the ground amplifies the exterior illumination.

Photograph: Nicholas Coates (2013).

appear less visible. Lighting the landscape from light poles reduced the interior reflections on the glass. This technique was also masterfully executed by lighting designer Richard Kelly at Johnson's Glass House, where the interior appears to be surrounded by walls of trees washed in spotlights (Figure 5.22).[60] By making the exterior brighter than the interior, a viewer inside is able to see through the glass without reflections obstructing the view. However, at Toledo, there are not sufficient vertical surfaces outside on which to project the light; the existing trees were too tall to be at eye level with the people inside. Consequently, the interior appears brighter and more visible at night than during the day.[61] The flickers of bright reflection spots on the glass play with the eyes to insinuate that there may be more glass rooms beyond a glass room, or perhaps it is a reflection of another.

In the daytime, the light in the courtyards provides additional natural illumination for the interior to balance out the light levels. Oki also noted that a high contrast of light levels and the constant views of reflections throughout the museum fatigue the eyes. The quiet, day-lit courtyards offer relief from the effects seen on glass (Figure 5.23).[62] Fierro describes a similar role served by the patio on the top floor of Nouvel's Institut du Monde Arabe: "the court relieves the tension of path otherwise unrelenting in its vertiginous

FIGURE 5.22 Lighting for the Glass House was designed by Richard Kelly. By washing the trees in spotlights, the interior appears to be surrounded by walls of trees.
Photograph: Steve Brosnahan (2007).

disorientation."[63] Although the effect of disorientation is more understated at Toledo, the courts in both buildings serve to alter the focus of the mind and the senses from the transparent glass. Whereas Nouvel's court provides a bird's-eye view of its urban context of Paris, Toledo's inner courtyards direct the gaze upward and downward: towards the sky framed by the curved openings and to the opaque white concrete pavement onto which the refracted and reflected light from the glass walls is projected. The natural light from the courts is filtered by curtains designed by Petra Blaisse's Amsterdam-based studio Inside Outside (Figure 5.24). The curtains are coated with reflective aluminum flakes on the exterior surface to both minimize solar gain and filter visible light, amplifying the diaphanous qualities of the interior.[64] The moveable curtains of the Toledo Pavilion recognize the variability of light on the building at different times of the year and day. Likewise, the transparency of the glass fluctuates with the season, the diurnal cycle, and the observer's position in relation to the glass walls.

Clear Glass Intensified

Observing the glass at the Toledo Glass Pavilion uncovers complex and intensified effects, as well as metaphysical readings of transparency. In the

FIGURE 5.23 Courtyard with framed view of the sky offers visual relief from the layered reflections on glass.

Photograph: Author (2012).

Pavilion, the execution of a novel plan and material organization is coalesced with skillful lamination and bending of glass and a daring approach to structural and mechanical engineering. It couples technical innovations with SANAA's intent to foreground the atmospheric effects over the structure by disrupting the conventional hierarchies between structure and partition, and concealment and exposure. From this approach emerges a different kind of intensified transparency of crystal clear glass. In the design process, the architects discovered unanticipated programmatic adjacencies afforded by transparent glass. Bubble-like glass rooms are connected to, yet isolated from, each other by an interstitial airspace typically concealed in an opaque *poché*. The air cavity appears to fluctuate in opacity and thickness, like the stroke of a brush. The effect is soft, fluid, and watery, evoking the return of glass to its nonrigid, liquid state, cushioned by air. The building is

FIGURE 5.24 The natural light from the courts is filtered by curtains coated with reflective aluminum flakes, designed by Inside Outside.

Photograph: Author (2012).

disciplined and precise in its execution, yet dynamic in sensual, intangible effects. In and around the Pavilion, the glass continuously presents views of the deep spaces beyond overlaid with reflections of locations far and near, through quick and slow motions. SANAA's spatial organization of program, materials, and light, combined with blurring of the opaque-transparent hier-archy in the structural and mechanical systems, results in a complex, intensi-fied space of perception and a novel interpretation of dynamic glass transparency.

Notes

1 Isobel Armstrong, *Victorian Glassworlds: Glass Culture and the Imagination 1830–1880* (Oxford: Oxford University Press, 2008), 4.

2 Ludwig Hilberseimer quoted in Terence Riley, *Light Construction* (New York: Museum of Modern Art, 2004), 10.

3 "History," Toledo Museum of Art, accessed July 29, 2016, www.toledomuseum. org/about/history/.

4 Toshihiro Oki, "The Glass Pavilion," in Michael Bell and Jeannie Kim, Eds., *Engineered Transparency: The Technical, Visual, and Spatial Effects of Glass* (New York: Princeton Architectural Press, 2011), 119.

5 Kazuyo Sejima, Yukio Futagawa, and Ryue Nishizawa, *Kazuyo Sejima, Ryue Nishizawa 2006–2011* (Tokyo: A.D.A. Edita, 2011), 23.

6 Tahree Lane, "Polishing the Glass Pavilion," *Blade*, June 4, 2006, accessed July 31, 2016, www.toledoblade.com/Art/2006/06/04/Polishing-the-Glass-Pavilion.html.

7 Oki, "The Glass Pavilion," 119.

8 Paul Scheerbart and Bruno Taut, *Glass Architecture, by Paul Scheerbart; and Alpine Architecture, by Bruno Taut* ed. Dennis Sharp (New York: Praeger, 1972), 122.

9 Armstrong, *Victorian Glassworlds*, 4–5. About 30% of glassmakers in Stourbridge, a center of British glassmaking during the Industrial Revolution, died before the age of 40, and about half died before 50.

10 Annette Fierro, *The Glass State: The Technology of the Spectacle, Paris, 1981–1998* (Cambridge: MIT Press, 2003), 117.

11 Toshihiro Oki, former project architect at SANAA on the Glass Pavilion at the Toledo Museum of Art, phone interview by author, January 8, 2017.

12 "Architecture," *Toledo Museum of Art*, accessed July 31, 2016, www.toledomuseum. org/glass-pavilion/architecture/.

13 Na Min Ra, principal in charge of the Glass Pavilion at glass consulting firm Front, phone interview by author, March 27, 2017.

14 Guy Nordenson and Brett Schneider, "Toledo Museum of Art Glass Pavilion," *Structure Magazine* (February 2009), 50–51, accessed July 25, 2016, www.structure mag.org/wp-content/uploads/2014/08/D-Spotlight-Nordenson-Feb-091.pdf.

15 Na Min Ra, principal in charge of the Glass Pavilion at glass consulting firm FRONT, email message to author, March 22, 2017.

16 Oki, interview.

17 Ra, interview.

18 Dietrich Neumann, "The Century's Triumph in Lighting: The Luxfer Prism Companies and Their Contribution to Early Modern Architecture," *Journal of the Society of Architectural Historians* 54, no. 1 (1995), 43, accessed July 22, 2016, www.jstor. org./stable/pdf/991024.pdf?_=1469308344047.

19 "Company History X," *Luxfer Gas Cylinders*, July 22, 2016, www.luxfercylinders. com/about/company-history.

20 Neumann, "The Century's Triumph in Lighting," 43.

21 Bernard Bauchet and Marc Vellay, "The Maison de Verre by Pierre Chareau," in Yukio Futagawa, Ed., *La Maison de Verre* (Tokyo: A.D.A. Edita, 1988), 11.

22 Reinhold Martin, *The Organizational Complex* (Cambridge: MIT Press, 2003).

23 Anthony Vidler, "Transparency," in *The Architectural Uncanny* (Cambridge: MIT Press, 1992), 219.

24 Vidler, *The Architectural Uncanny*, 219.

25 Vidler, *The Architectural Uncanny*, 221.

26 Toshiko Mori curated the exhibition *Immaterial/Ultramaterial* at Harvard GSD in 2001. Michael Bell organized the multi-year Columbia Conference on Architecture, Engineering and Materials starting in 2008.

27 Riley, *Light Construction*, 9–10.
28 Ufuk Ersoy, "Glass, as Light as Air, as Deep as Water," in Matthew Mindrup, Ed., *Material Imagination: Reveries on Architecture and Matter* (Burlington, VT: Ashgate, 2015), 156.
29 Scheerbart, *Glass Architecture*, 14.
30 Scheerbart, *Glass Architecture*, 42.
31 Scheerbart, *Glass Architecture*, 42.
32 Vanessa Fernandez, "Preservation of Modern-Era Office Buildings and Their Environmental Controls," *APT Bulletin* 42, no. 2/3, 21–22.
33 Josh Barbanel, "Study: Glass Condos Could Pose Health Threat Through Overheating," *The Wall Street Journal*, February 2, 2014, accessed July 25, 2016, www.wsj.com/articles/SB10001424052702304428004579350881672554084.
34 Kiel Moe, *Integrated Design in Contemporary Architecture* (New York: Princeton Architectural Press, 2008), 106.
35 Moe, *Integrated Design*, 106.
36 Ra, interview.
37 Cristina Diaz Moreno and Efren Garcia Grinda, "Ocean of Air," in Richard C. Levene and Fernando Márquez Cecilia, Eds., *SANAA Sejima Nishizawa 1983–2004 (El Croquis,* 121–122 (2004), 26–39).
38 Oki, interview.
39 Nordenson and Schneider, "Toledo Museum of Art Glass Pavilion.".
40 Moreno and Grinda, "Ocean of Air," 374.
41 Fierro, *The Glass State*, 100.
42 Kenneth Frampton, "The Glass House Revisited," in Jeffrey Kipnis and David Whitney, Eds., *Philip Johnson: The Glass House* (New York: Pantheon, 1983), 105. First published in *Catalog 9*, September/October 1978.
43 Ashley R. Wilson of Graham Gund Architect, trust architect responsible for the glass at both Philip Johnson's Glass House and Mies's Farnsworth House, email to author, August 7, 2019. According to Wilson, the Glass House's panels have been replaced over the last 70 years with various types, ranging from quarter-inch to three-eighth-inch annealed, heat strengthened, or fully tempered. At Farnsworth, the replacements are three-eighth-inch tempered. Tempered glass tends to have noticeable distortions.
44 Wilson, email.
45 Davidson Norris, glass and daylight consultant with Carpenter Norris Consulting, email to author, August 7, 2019.
46 Frampton, "The Glass House Revisited," 94.
47 Alejandro Zaera-Polo with Kazuyo Sejima and Ryue Nishizawa, "A Conversation," in Richard C. Levene and Fernando Márquez Cecilia, Eds., *SANAA Sejima Nishizawa 1983–2004 (El Croquis,* 121–122 (2004), 18).
48 Ákos Moravánszky, "Mies-en-scène," in Xavier Costa, Ed., *SANAA: Kazuyo Sejima, Ryue Nishizawa* (Barcelona: Actar, 2010), 33.
49 Richard H. Putney and Paula Reich, *Glass in Glass* (Toledo, OH: Toledo Museum of Art, 2012), 10.
50 Lane, "Polishing the Glass Pavilion."
51 Ra, interview.
52 Oki, interview.
53 Oki, interview.
54 Nordenson and Schneider, "Toledo Museum of Art Glass Pavilion,"50.
55 Toyo Ito, "Diagram Architecture," in Kazuyo Sejima et al., Eds., *Kazuyo Sejima + Ryue Nishizawa (El Croquis,* 2000), 331.
56 Oki, interview.

57 Beatriz Colomina, "Undisturbed," in Xavier Costa, Ed., *SANAA: Kazuyo Sejima, Ryue Nishizawa* (Barcelona: Actar, 2010), 29.
58 Oki, Interview.
59 Oki, Interview.
60 Arthur Drexler, "The Architecture Opaque and Transparent," in Jeffrey Kipnis and David Whitney, Eds., *Philip Johnson: The Glass House* (New York: Pantheon, 1983), 5.
61 Oki, Interview.
62 Oki, Interview.
63 Fierro, *The Glass State*, 141.
64 Moe, *Integrated Design*, 106.

6

IMPERMANENT MONUMENT FOR INTIMATE MACHINES
Apple's Glass Cube

Glass as an architectural material has become fundamentally linked with Apple's products and architecture, so much so that Apple refers metonymically to their iPhone by its material: "It's a piece of glass for Apple to deliver its exciting new software," said a senior vice president of marketing.[1] In 2007, Apple launched its first iPhone with a monolithic glass touch screen, breaking away from the mechanical keyboards of smartphone competitors such as BlackBerry and Nokia. Through finger taps and swipes, the glass interface has shortened the distance between humans and machines; glass is the medium through which most intimate news secrets and images are exchanged. Apple's emblematic application of glass extends beyond their products. From the Apple retail stores' structural glass stairs, to the ultrathin, chemically strengthened Gorilla® Glass on the iPhone screen, the Apple brand is associated with high-strength glass in ways that defy the conventional association of fragility to glass. Apple's architecture first deployed high-tech glass in 2002 at its New York flagship store in SoHo. It showcased all-glass stairs in which the treads and walls were laminated with hurricane- and bullet-resistant ionoplast interlayers. On the one hand, transparent glass is an ironic material choice for a company known for its culture of secrecy. On the other hand, glass is an apt symbolism for a company whose products are profoundly linked with the material. If aluminum was the material of the jet age, glass is the material of the information age, in which light signals are transmitted through pure glass strands about the diameter of human hair.

Apple has effectively ascribed glass's symbolism of perfection to its products and architecture. In 1935, Le Corbusier writes that glass is imbued with a sense of perfection:

Glass that allows total light penetration, passing through without any distortion. Glass that, from inside the building, is as pure as a clear sky and that, from outside, provides distinct angles, a sense of flow, brilliance, and fluid movement. Glass that gives a sense of perfection. What a wonderful material to perfectly express part of the spirit of Modern Age![2]

While this particular modern association with glass prevails, the material properties of glass architecture have transformed. In Le Corbusier's time, glass could only be an infill for a window framed by steel, wood, or concrete. With the Apple cube, transparent glass serves as the structural walls and beams that let in light and view, thereby calling into question basic elements of architecture. Likewise, cultural meanings associated with transparent glass must also be reconsidered when questioning what constitutes monumentality in architecture.

Of Apple's numerous transparent structures, the store on Manhattan's 5th Avenue (Figure 6.1) draws attention to its striking all-glass cube. Designed by architects Bohlin Cywinski Jackson (BCJ), structural engineers Eckersley O'Callaghan

FIGURE 6.1 Apple's glass cube, designed by architects Bohlin Cywinski Jackson, on the northeast corner plaza of 5th Avenue and 59th Street in Manhattan. The cube serves as the vestibule to the retail store below.

Photograph: Peter Aaron (2006).

(EOC),[3] and Steve Jobs and opened in 2006, the cube has attained the qualities of monumental architecture given its relatively small size and retail store function. It is the fifth most photographed landmark in New York City, surpassed only by the Empire State Building, Times Square, the Rockefeller Center, and Grand Central Station,[4] all of which are – even though they too symbolize American commerce – generally more accepted as monuments than the computer retail store. Since the store's opening in 2006, the glass cube has been ritualistically reconstructed three times, then ceremoniously revealed, as if it were the launch of a new Apple product. The process resembles the ritualistic replacement of a fully functional, two-year-old iPhone with a new version that is faster, smarter, and features commands that were previously unimaginable. Each version of the phone is highly anticipated and ceremoniously revealed to a massive audience.

This chapter explores the material and meaning in Apple's glass cube, a monument made of an immaterial material that is at once both ephemeral and robust, transparent and conspicuous. These characteristics contradict conventional associations of monuments with permanent, opaque materials, such as stone and concrete. How does the glass cube embody the sometimes conflicting characteristics and qualities of an architectural monument? This chapter argues that glass is an appropriate material choice for a monument in the information age.

The Magic of Glass

As Henry Urbach, the former director of the Glass House in New Canaan, writes, Apple's architecture inspires awe:

> Quasi-religious in almost every respect, Apple stores are chapels for the Information Age. They reproduce something of the hush and reverence associated with traditional space of worship, offering a rarified atmosphere for individuals to commune with the gods of advanced technology. Individual dreams, hopes, and fantasies – a yearning for *bildung*, for self-actualization and betterment – come to life here.[5]

The symbolic associations of glass, as well as its material properties, engender this aura. A nearly magical quality has been associated with glass historically. "Its visible invisibility is what is important about [glass] transparency. It must be both a barrier and medium. The riddles it proposes arise from the logic of its material and sensuous nature,"[6] writes Isobel Armstrong, a British scholar and critic of 19th century literature. From the 11th to the 16th century, the Venetian Republic held a monopoly in the production of glass, until the Minister of Finance under Louis the XIV lured Italian glassworkers to France to make mirrors for Versailles. Glass and glassmakers' skills were highly prized. According to legend, infuriated Venetians sent agents to France to poison the glassworkers to keep the trade a secret. As art historian Rosemarie Haag Bletter writes, because of glass's preciousness in preindustrial periods, coupled with its brittleness, glass appeared frequently in architectural fantasies, in the "realm of wishful thinking."[7] Apple is known for making a fantasy-like machine a reality, so realizing the dream of an all-glass building appears to be an apt challenge for the company.

British structural engineer James O'Callaghan, who co-founded the engineering firm EOC in 2004, began collaborating with Steve Jobs and BCJ on Apple's glass architecture in 2001, while working for engineering firm Dewhurst Macfarlane & Partners (DMP).[8] O'Callaghan first presented the design of glass stairs, which featured all-glass stair treads supported by a metal rail system, at the Apple flagship store in SoHo. To this proposal, Jobs responded, "I think you should make it (the stair) all out of glass."[9] In a characteristic Jobs manner, he demanded a design that is streamlined, like an iPod that has one button instead of several. Jobs's repeated call to simplify design underpinned Apple's identity. The provocation to make all-glass stairs launched O'Callaghan, BCJ, and TriPyramid's ongoing design collaboration on Apple's iconic store architecture, which showcases trademark glass stair, roof, and storefront design that minimizes connections in size and frequency, and maximizes glass panel sizes.[10] According to O'Callaghan, the initial concept of the SoHo store glass stairs was to create a structure that "would allow maximum transparency through the space and not detract customers' views of the products displayed."[11] Apple also insisted on not only a functional but a "magical" structure that would awe. O'Callaghan suggested that a "magical" structure would be possible with spanning elements made only in glass, connected with discrete metal fittings.[12] The fittings were designed with and manufactured by TriPyramid Structures, a high-precision metal hardware design and fabrication company who applied knowledge from the rigging technology of high performance yachts to the hardware of the Louvre Pyramid.

In the Apple Stores, the omnipresent glass in the architecture, display cases, and the display screens amplifies the enchanted qualities of the products. Similar to Victorian storefronts in Europe in late-19th century cities, Apple has revealed the presence of glass as a material. Throughout the ages, transparent glass has not been invisible; in fact, it is present and conspicuous. The magical imagery of glass – as a substance simultaneously present and absent – underlies its use in stories, especially fairy tales. For example, in the story of Cinderella, glass becomes the founding element of the story. Armstrong writes, "it was essential that the glass slipper fitted the right person – and Cinderella's magical transformation became mediated by glass."[13] In Lewis Carroll's *Through the Looking-Glass,* Alice finds a fantastical world on the other side of the mirror above the mantle (Figure 6.2). In this alternative world, like a mirror reflection, logics are reversed. "Jabberwocky," an epic poem in the story, can only be read reflected in a mirror. Alice runs to slow down. Tweedledum and

FIGURE 6.2 In Lewis Carroll's *Through the Looking-Glass*, Alice finds a fantastical world on the other side of the mirror above the mantle.

Illustration: John Tenniel (1871).

Tweedledee are rotund, fictional men who are identical except that they are mirror images of each other. In fairy tales, glass and mirror, with their mutable qualities, offer glimpses into an alternative, magical world. Glass, whether by transmitting light through itself or reflecting light, becomes a doorway to another domain, a spirit world of light. Similarly, the all-glass stairs and the cube transition consumers from the world of everyday to one tinged with a seductive otherworldliness (Figure 6.3).

The Cube's Three Iterations

The cube measures 32 feet and 6 inches on each side and height, with a 10 foot-10 inch square opening for doors and side panels centered on the 5th Avenue side. This door is connected by a glass bridge to the spiral stairs. In all three versions of the cube constructed in 2006, 2011, and 2019, certain aspects remain unchanged: the location, function, and overall dimensions (Figures 6.4 and 6.5). The cube anchors a prominent location in New York City: the GM Plaza at the southeast corner of Central Park announcing where 5th Avenue shifts from a retail street to the south, to the park with its museums to the north. The cube – with its freestanding, platonic form rendered in crystalline glass – serves as a strikingly monumental entrance to the retail store below, which remains unseen from street level except for the cylindrical glass elevator enclosure. An unmistakable precedent is I. M. Pei's Louvre Pyramid (1989)

FIGURE 6.3 The all-glass stairs and the cube transition consumers from the world of the everyday to one tinged with a seductive otherworldliness.

Photograph: Peter Aaron/OTTO (2011).

FIGURE 6.4 Apple's 2006 cube with 90 panels.

Photograph: Mike Cotter.

FIGURE 6.5   Apple's 2011 cube with 15 panels.

Photograph: Peter Aaron.

(Figure 6.6), another platonic glass structure that serves as an entrance vestibule and brings light to the basement floor below. Peter Bohlin sketched the idea for the Apple cube during a meeting with Jobs.[14] The cube, which Bernard Cywinski calls a "ceremony of descent,"[15] acts as a striking vestibule on a prominent intersection, publicly imposing its power and authority. Customers enters the cube facing the GM building and, as they step down the central spiral stairs, are presented with a panorama of the iconic intersection. The streetscape disappears entirely from view upon descent and, once at the store level, Apple products and the store experience hypnotically capture consumers' attention.

The original cube (2006) comprised 90 panels of glass, with 5 foot-5 inch by 10 foot-10 inch vertical panels and 5 foot-5inch square roof panels. The structure was formed with vertical glass fins placed 5-feet 5-inches apart on all four sides. Each fin consists of five layers of half-inch thick heat-strengthened glass laminated to form a single piece. These fins support a roof lattice of criss-crossed three-ply laminated glass beams.[16] This roof is based on a lamellar principal, which was developed in Germany in the 1920s to build long-span structures by interlocking short wood beams.[17] Because of the material's strength, the cube's glass roof system requires no moment connection, which minimizes joints, further amplifying the illusion of the roof floating atop glass fins.

FIGURE 6.6   The Louvre Pyramid, a platonic glass structure that serves as an entrance vestibule and brings light to the basement floor below.

Photograph: Author (2018).

In 2011, Apple revealed its second version of the cube, following much anticipation, just as with the launch of a new iPhone. The construction site was concealed by unnecessarily tall temporary plywood walls to heighten expectations. The walls were painted, exhibiting simple, white-on-gray line drawings of the new and the old cubes (Figure 6.7), as if the engineering drawings were released before the product. The text below the illustration reads: "We're simplifying the Fifth Avenue cube. By using larger, seamless pieces of glass, we're just using 15 panes instead of 90."[18] The second cube's (2011) panels, 10 foot-10inch by 32 foot-6inch of five-ply glass, were laminated SentryGlas®, the hurricane- and bullet-resistant ionoplast[19] interlayer initially developed by Dupont and currently owned by Japanese synthetic fiber company Kuraray. The word "glas" in its trade name is misleading, since it is the ionoplast – a plastic, not glass – that gives stiffness. Developed as a hurricane-proof glass solution and approved to meet the stringent Miami-Dade County building code, ionoplast interlayer is a hundred times stiffer than the commonly used polyvinyl butyral (PVB) interlayer and higher in bond strength. In case of breakage, the stiffness of the glass–plastic laminate helps to hold the structure in place. For instance, when a heavy object crashes into a frameless glass balustrade laminated with a PVB interlayer, the broken glass pieces will stay together adhered to the interlayer, but the glass sheet will lose

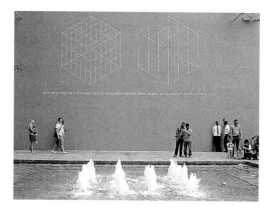

FIGURE 6.7 The glass cube was temporarily shrouded in plywood painted in gray, with white line drawings of the new and the old cubes. Underneath, the caption reads, "We're simplifying the Fifth Avenue cube. By using larger, seamless pieces of glass, we're just using 15 panes instead of 90."

Photograph: Noel Y. Calingasan (August 2011).

stiffness and drape like a curtain over the floor edge. In contrast, a glass balustrade laminated with an ionoplast interlayer will maintain stiffness and remain upright to protect people from falling, and keep the broken pieces of glass adhered as a single panel. Ionoplast interlayer, when heated in autoclave for lamination, flows seamlessly around metal inserts sandwiched between sheets of glass, thus forming a tighter bond. With a higher adherence of ionoplast interlayer, a metal hardware laminated between sheets of glass will more likely stay in place, without sliding or dislodging.

While the perception of glass transparency can be manipulated in a variety of ways, the cube does this by reducing the number of fittings and using larger glass panels. According to O'Callaghan, "The success of [a] glass structure is, in my opinion, a function of the elegance of its connectivity. The transparency is defined by the frequency of the fittings."[20] The Apple Store's second cube, built with lamination interlayers with greater stiffness and adherence, has far fewer seams and metal hardware connections than its predecessor (Figure 6.8). As joints between materials are reduced to the minimum, the cube becomes even more conspicuous. On the other hand, the first cube, with a higher number of glass pieces and consequently more exposed edges, sparkled more. The polished edges of glass are arrised, or chambered about one-sixteenth of an inch at a 45-degree angle, which make them act as tiny prisms that shine while separating light into component colors. Although it sparkles less, the new crystalline cube appears to magically stand without the structural supports found in conventional glass architecture, such as steel columns, beams, or walls. In this version of "less is more," fewer joints and material types deliver a monumental impact.

FIGURE 6.8 Metal hardware is reduced in dimension in the new iteration. Roof beam saddle hardware details from first (left) and second (right) versions of the cube. Photograph: TriPyramid Structures (left: 2006 and right: 2011).

Most recently, as from January 2017, the cube has been on "sabbatical," as Apple hired Foster and Partners to redesign and expand the retail space underneath from 32,000 to 77,000 square feet.[21] The building permit approves a "full removal of glass cubical structure at Apple store entrance"[22] as a necessary part of the basement store expansion. In the new scheme, the basement is lit with natural daylight from skylights which are visible on the 5th Avenue plaza.[23] As a part of this extensive expansion and renovation, the cube was returned to its place in June of 2018, and was scheduled to reopen that November (Figure 6.9).[24] In each reconstruction, neither the footprint nor the function of the cube has changed. During the second iteration, only the joint details, panel sizes, and engineering of the glass were updated with newly tested materials and techniques. The third cube is built to the exact same specification as the second cube, but using all newly fabricated parts. The cost to disassemble and reassemble the existing cube with New York City union labor would have exceeded the cost to rebuild with all new parts. Additionally, in the third cube, longer metal stairs will replace the glass spiral stairs to accommodate the new basement ceiling height that is 10 feet higher than previously.[25]

FIGURE 6.9 The 5th Avenue Apple Store under renovation in July 2019. The third cube is a reconstruction of the second cube, with the exact same specification but with all glass and metal newly fabricated. The cube is protected with sheathing until the basement retail store renovation is complete.

Photograph: Author (2019).

This approach to attaining permanence – by reproducing the same design with continual replacement of parts – is analogous to the Japanese attitude towards building preservation. The ancient Ise Shrine has been reconstructed to the exact specification of materials and details every 20 years for the past 2,000 years. The Ise Shrine honors the Shinto notion of impermanence of all things by means of cyclical death and renewal. A modern example of this approach is the Metabolism, a thread of Japanese modernism that promoted a living, changing architecture through continual renewal and expansion. The Nakagin Capsule Tower (1972) by Kisho Kurokawa is an iconic example of Metabolism. The architect intended the capsules to be replaced every 25 years, updating the materials and technology to reflect current society at each rebirth, while the concrete circulation core and the structure remain unchanged.[26] The cube's analogy to Metabolist architecture suggests that Jobs perhaps wished for the cube to live in perpetuity through continuous renewal.

Fragile yet Robust

The glass used in the cube, as well as in other hallmark glass structures in Apple retail stores, is exceptionally shatter-resistant. Glass is associated with material vulnerability; broken glasses or cracked window panes are common sights in everyday life. Yet, Apple glass structures continue to underscore the increasing structural strength of glass. This strength comes not from the material of glass itself, but from newly tested glass engineering knowledge coupled with innovations in plastic interlayers, metal hardware, and the fusion of these three materials – both literally and figuratively. In the past two decades, structural glass beams, made by laminating glass sheets with a plastic interlayer, have expanded the possibilities of long-span glass structures.[27] This technological concept borrowed from laminated wood beams and plywood sheets was applied to glass. The newly developed ionoplast sheets fuse multiple sheets of glass into exceptionally stiff structural panels. This synthesis minimizes deflection and counters glass's inherent tendency to shatter in tension.

Whereas glass stairs conventionally rely on steel beams, stringers, and columns for structural support, the original SoHo Apple Store stairs of 2002 were designed with all-glass balustrades and treads, in which all primary loads were carried by glass.[28] The treads consisted of four layers of annealed glass[29] adhered together with three sheets of plastic interlayers. These stairs made two notable advancements in structural glass: the use of ionoplast interlayer, which has a greater stiffness and bond strength

FIGURE 6.10 The second version of the SoHo Apple Store glass stairs.

Photograph: TriPyramid Structures (2011).

than its predecessor the PVB interlayer, and the embedding of metal hardware in between sheets of glass using the high adhesive properties of ionoplast (Figure 6.10).[30] These metal inserts would allow glass panels to mechanically fasten to each other. The only metal pieces in the treads were hardware about the size of a halved hockey puck. The glass treads connected to glass rails with computer numerical control (CNC)-milled stainless steel and titanium hardware laminated between sheets of glass. The high bond strength of interlayer meant that in the case of glass breakage, the laminated tread would remain stiff and not fall out of place. Another staircase for the Los Angeles store followed shortly after the New York store, demonstrating that all-glass stairs could meet significant seismic loads when the structure is hung, rather than supported at its base.[31]

Ten years after the SoHo stairs' initial construction, the stairs were redesigned in 2012 to further push the limits of glass fabrication and hardware design; they were reconstructed using fewer, larger glass walls, four instead of three layers of interlayer for higher stiffness, and even more discreet metal hardware (Figure 6.11).[32] Despite the high stiffness and bond strength of ionoplast interlayer that can make laminated glass assembly more robust, glass is not shatterproof. During a snowstorm in January 2014, a snowplow accidentally knocked into the cube, shattering a 32.5-foot

FIGURE 6.11 In the second version, each tread consists of five glass sheets laminated with ionoplast interlayer. CNC-milled stainless and titanium semicircular hardware is laminated between sheets of glass. The hardware is mechanically fasted to a hockey puck-sized cylinder, which attaches the treads to the single-piece glass balustrades.
Photograph: TriPyramid Structures (2011).

panel, which allegedly resulted in nearly half a million-dollars' worth of damage.[33] Like a shattered iPhone glass screen, damaged glass comes with a great price. The replacement cost of a damaged iPhone screen costs as much as $329 for the newest iPhone XS Max.[34,35] Despite the associated risks, glass tempts consumers and clients to pay its high price. Like Narcissus who was fatally seduced by his own reflection on the water, glass continues to allure.

Refining Glass Production

Apple glass architecture is symbolically linked to a hallmark of all Apple products: the ultrathin glass screens that protect and act as an interface between people and machines, and between the actual and the virtual worlds. In 2006, Steve Jobs approached Corning Glass to make thin sheets of unbreakable glass, giving them six months to develop it for the 2007 iPhone launch.[36] In response, Corning delivered Gorilla® Glass, a chemically strengthened glass with a thickness of less than 1 mm. Glass cracks generally start from flaws on the glass surface. Thus, in order to prevent breakage, flaws – including microscopic scratches or chips – must be eliminated during the production process. Gorilla® Glass is strengthened by creating a deep compression layer on the surface of the glass, thereby significantly reducing imperfections.[37] Whereas the tempering process similarly creates a compressive layer on the surface by raising the temperature, then quickly lowering it (called "quenching"), Gorilla® Glass instead uses a chemical that causes an ion-exchange process.

Over the past 160 years, glass production processes have progressed rapidly, reducing flaws and increasing product versatility. The glass sheets in the Crystal Palace (1851) were made by men who blew air from their lungs into glass balls which were made into cylinders, sliced open, then ground and polished to make flat glass. Imperfections from uneven airflow, or debris in the air, resulted in numerous imperfections and ripples, making them vulnerable to breakage. In 1952, Alastair Pilkington invented the float glass manufacturing method, in which molten glass is poured onto a bath of molten tin to make thin, flat surfaces.[38] Although a significant improvement from blown glass, even small particles of debris in the tin bath can result in imperfect surfaces. Gorilla® Glass is made with the fusion process, a method in which molten glass is drawn downward from a v-shaped trough to make ultrathin glass.[39] These flawless sheets are between 1 and 4 mm thick in Gorilla® Glass, and are 100 microns for the even thinner Willow® Glass. Apple's products' success has depended on refining and protecting the material properties of glass. Apple's use of glass distinguishes them from their competitors, in both the streamlined aesthetics and the scratch resistance of their display screens; it seems fitting then, that Apple's architecture is built with the material that symbolizes their achievement.

The Cube's Monumentality

Definitions of monumentality in architecture indicate a variety of factors, from the structure's size and innovations in construction materials and techniques, to the civic values for which it stands. Some definitions of monumentality are even contradictory. Perhaps the most widespread idea about monumentality is that it has to be a very large size. Although a 32.5-foot cube is dwarfed in size compared to other familiar monumental architecture, such as the Great Pyramid of Giza (originally 481 feet tall),[40] or even other iconic glass monuments such as the Louvre Pyramid (72 feet tall), the cube exemplifies multiple definitions of monumental architecture. The cube's materiality suggests a new type of monument appropriate for its time and purpose, made with a substance not traditionally associated with monuments.

Monuments as Symbols of Human Aims

In the 20th century, architects largely turned away from monumentality, as an outdated interest of traditional architecture, to instead focus on the social functioning of buildings. When modern architects posed the question of monumentality, it was seen afresh. In 1943, urban planner Josep L. Sert, painter Ferdinand Leger, and architecture historian Sigfried Giedion wrote the essay "Nine Points on Monumentality." Of the nine, two are elaborated here in order to understand how the Apple cube aligns with Western definitions of monumentality. The first point states, "Monuments are human landmarks which men have created as symbols for their ideals, for their aims, and for their actions. They are intended to outlive the period which originated them, and constitute a heritage for future generations."[41]

In the case of Apple, the cube symbolizes the spirit behind their products, which is connected to the public persona of Steve Jobs. The mourning that followed the death of Jobs was akin to that of civic heroes, like Martin Luther King Junior, John Lennon, and John F. Kennedy. However, unlike these men, Jobs was not known for his likability, generosity, or ethical ways; in fact, he had a reputation for arrogance and ruthlessness. Why, then, would masses of strangers congregate at Apple retail stores worldwide to mourn his death? One possibility is that the mourning was for the company, and its leader, who brought them products that somehow defined an identity of the time – the intimate machines of iPhones, iPods, and iPads.[42] These devices are a means to the human aims of self-expression and connection with other people.

In smartphones, glass is the surface of human contact with the machine. Intimate information – from photos of family and pets that bring joy and texts that make our hearts race, to recorded voices that make our hearts sink – is all accessed through the touch of fingertips on glass. Intuitive commands that use fingers – from tap and swipe, to zoom – heighten the intimacy between the devices and our minds and bodies. Despite criticisms against technology in the information age, including alienation, loss of privacy, and a variety of ailments resulting from addiction to devices, mobile phones have undeniably transformed the ways people express themselves and connect with each other. We increasingly receive the important stories of our lives – from those of births, deaths, and engagements, to victories and losses in elections – through the light-emitting glass screens of our phones. Glass is the mediator of our most intimate secrets and news. Glass, then, is a fitting material choice for a monument to Apple's intimate machines.

In a 1995 interview, Steve Jobs was asked whether he was a "hippy or a nerd," and he responded he was clearly a hippy, for the spark and the spirit that the hippies sought out:

> (The spirit) is the same thing that causes people to want to be poets instead of bankers, and I think that's a wonderful thing. I think that same spirit can be put into products. Those products can be manufactured and given to people, and they can sense that spirit. If you talk to people that use the Macintosh, they love it. You don't hear of people loving products very often, but you could really feel it.[43]

This spirit at the core of Apple's design and marketing, one that elicits intimacy between people and their devices, may be what stirred sympathy in Apple fans worldwide. Jobs also spoke about the humanist side of Apple's design, which other tech companies cannot seem to master:

> The whole computer industry wants to forget about the humanist side and just focus on the technology. But I think there's a whole other side of the coin, which is, "What do we do with these things?" "Can we do more than spreadsheets and word processors?" "Can we help you express yourself in richer ways?"[44]

Apple claims to shorten the distance between humans and machines by making personal computing apparently *personal*. The iPhone emphasizes the "I" – reference to a self[45] – fulfilling human needs for emotional and intellectual connections. This apparent, or real, intimacy, and the surge of the feel-good hormone dopamine caused by what the screen delivers, are also what makes smartphones addictive.

While glass aptly symbolizes Apple in many ways, there is also an irony to Apple's choice of transparent glass to symbolize their company. Apple is known for its culture of secrecy, where employees are prohibited to talk about the company or their products. Apple's product launches rely on intense concealment and the big reveal that follows. Tellingly, the transparent glass cube on 5th Avenue most prominently frames its glowing logo (Figure 6.1). The cube is the rhetorical devise, and the store with products, employees, and customers is hidden underneath. Despite the contradiction between the clear visual appearance of glass and the opaque company culture, the cube is a profoundly effective symbol for a company that has shortened the distance between humans and machines through a glass interface.

Monuments Built with Cutting-Edge Technology

In addition to symbolizing human aims, a monument, according to Giedion, Leger and Sert, must be built using cutting-edge materials and techniques.[46] When the essay was written in 1942, materials such as light metal, laminated wood arches, and metal trusses enabled long spans of monumental scale. Similarly, the Apple cube uses the latest glass engineering, materials, and fabrication techniques to make a building that awes. The cube is a nearly all-glass structure. The prefabricated glass panels with metal joints are bolted together on site, and the seams between the glass sheets are sealed with silicone caulk, recessed slightly from the surface to remain as unobtrusive as possible. A decade of ongoing collaborations between Apple, structural engineers, and glass fabricators generated technical expertise and the confidence to push the limits of glass. The Apple cube required that the German glass supplier Bischoff Glass Technologies (BGT) and the contractor Seele GmbH fabricate oversized glass fins 32 feet-6 inches long. The existing autoclave could only accommodate up to 20 feet. To meet this challenge, BGT and Seele worked with EOC to develop a way to laminate glass fins in staggered lengths so that they could be mechanically spliced. After building the first cube, BGT and Seele found an aircraft manufacturer who, during downtime, would let them use their aircraft wing autoclave to laminate large panels of glass, with successful results.[47] For the Apple Stores in Boston and Sydney (2008), Seele purchased an autoclave that could laminated panels up to 46 feet high. Following the success of these projects, Jobs asked BCJ what could be done with the cube, then insisted on rebuilding the cube with larger panels, which Apple did in 2012 using Seele's autoclave.[48,49] These incremental developments that constantly meet increasing demands further contribute to the monumentality of Apple's cube. Simultaneously, Apple's iterative developments in glass have helped to prove that glass can now be a primary material for monumental architecture, as stone and concrete could in prior generations.

Thermodynamic Definition of Monumentality

Monumentality is not only contingent on the most advanced forms of technologies but also on the power and influence necessary to fulfil monumental tasks. According to a thermodynamic explanation of monumentality, archaeologist Bruce Trigger argues,

> In human societies, the control of energy constitutes [a] fundamental and universally recognized measure of political power. The most basic way in which power can be symbolically reinforced is through the conspicuous consumption of energy. Monumental architecture, as a highly visible and enduring form of such consumption, plays an important role in shaping the political and economic behavior of human beings.[50]

Only a powerful brand like Apple could move fabricators and manufacturers to realize such an ambitious project. In addition to laminating glass with an aircraft wing autoclave, Beijing North Glass (BNG) in China invested six months of research to build a tempering machine large enough to temper 46-foot glass panels for Apple. Besides the size increase, BNG, which was accustomed to prioritizing speed over quality, had to meet the highest quality and precision that Apple demanded. With the new machine, BNG fabricated 41-foot curved glass for the glass drum at Apple IFC Shanghai.[51] By controlling the materials and specialized skills, Apple creates structures that impress, which in turn motivates their collaborators to expand their capabilities; Apple's brand influences company behaviors with its awe-inspiring presence. The reach extends beyond the company to enable success through partnerships, including the development of Gorilla® Glass by Corning and advancements in structural glass engineering.

There are other measures of Apple and Steve Jobs's political and financial powers. First is the real estate deal Jobs negotiated with Harry Macklowe, the landlord of the GM Building and its plaza where the cube is located (Figure 6.12). In 2003, Macklowe purchased the GM Building for $1.4 billion. The iconic 50-story skyscraper was designed by Edward Durrell Stone & Associates and Emery Roth & Sons and completed in 1968. Macklowe knew that the

FIGURE 6.12 The cube became a solution to the underused public plaza of the GM Building to the right.

Photograph: Peter Aaron/OTTO (2006).

building had two problems: its underused public plaza extending between the building's entry lobby and the street corner, and the basement retail space. Convinced that the Apple retail store would be the solution to his real estate problems, he repeatedly approached Apple's vice president of real estate. Steve Jobs had returned to Apple as the CEO in 1996 and had launched the iPod in 2001, but had not yet released the iPhone (2007). Apple was looking to position itself as the undisputable leader in the consumer electronics retail scene, and Macklowe owned the potential retail space. In November 2003, Macklowe was invited to a meeting with Jobs and the lead architect Peter Bohlin in Cupertino.[52] Jobs presented the idea of a glass cube on the public plaza, with an underground retail store open 24/7. "It took us half an hour to make a deal,"[53] said Macklowe. However, the 20-year lease includes an unusual agreement: that Steve Jobs could take the $9 million cube with him upon expiration of the lease.[54] Apple's power to influence business transactions underscores the cube's monumentality.

Second, Steve Jobs and other members of the cube's design team hold a patent on the cube's design.[55] While patents are customary in the field of product design, they are nearly nonexistent in architecture. In fact, patent number US D712,067 S, filed for the second version of the cube, shows the glass cube with no foundation or site, as if it were a product – a piece of technology – rather than a building. Akin to Kenneth Frampton's characterization of Maison de Verre as an enlarged piece of furniture inserted in an 18th-century residential building,[56] the cube may be understood as a piece of glass technology inserted into the plaza. Approved by the US Patent and Trademark Office in August 2014, it lists the seven inventors of the cube, including the architects, engineer, and Steve Jobs. The document comprises six pages, five of which are simple line drawings of the cube, and text is strikingly absent. To indicate transparent glass in the elevation drawings, the illustrator used short, parallel diagonal lines, an architectural convention for showing glass. A note on the first page of the patent reads, "The oblique lines in the Figures show transparency and not surface ornamentation."[57] The extraordinary engineering, business acumen, and political maneuvering required for this monumental project strikingly contrast the minimal lines in the drawings and the brevity of the patent. This design patent, which protects the appearance of the cube but says nothing about how it functions (which a utility patent would protect), is consistent with Apple's approach to intellectual property protection for their products. In the 2016 lawsuit Apple vs. Samsung, Apple was awarded over $500 million for Samsung's infringement on their smartphone design appearance.[58] Paying the significant cost associated with protection of intellectual property is a part of Apple's business strategy. The cube's patent is another evidence of their power, which further reinforces the cube's monumentality.

Moreover, it seems improbable for Apple and a designer other than Jobs to obtain a patent for a building that, despite its striking appearance, uses building technologies that are not unprecedented. By 2014, there were a number of buildings that used structural glass laminated with ionoplast interlayer, including the cable net glass wall at the Time Warner Center, on the opposite corner of Central Park South, by SOM and James Carpenter Design Associates. The idea of a platonic glass structure as a vestibule had already been built by I. M. Pei. This further proves that it is Apple's power to make things happen that amplifies the cube's monumentality.

Redefining the Monument for Modern Times

In 1937, Lewis Mumford declared in "The Death of the Monument," that permanent monuments are inappropriate for modern culture:

> The protective function of the city, tendencies toward fixities and permanence of function, have been overdone: for a living creature the only real protection and permanence comes through growth and renewal and reproduction: processes which are precisely the opposite of petrifaction.[59]

Cecil Elliot, in his 1964 essay "Monuments and Monumentality," responds to Mumford's proclamation and reexamines modern monumentality. He writes that, before a monument is built, there must be a general belief in the lasting significance of the person or event to which it is dedicated. A monument "necessarily presupposes that its meaning will endure."[60] While this definition is similar to those offered by Giedion and others, Elliot writes that whereas permanence was a requirement for a monument in the past, material and economic factors acutely limit the expected life span of buildings. In contrast to the pre-modern monuments, he claims, "Permanence is an exceptional requirement ... New materials must slowly gain acceptance as suited to monuments."[61] Due to its brittleness, glass was not understood as a primary building material in monuments until the latter half of the 1900s. Joseph Paxton's Crystal Palace of 1851 is monumental in its size, long span, and spectacular technical ambitions. However, a fire in 1936 – either caused by the wood flooring catching cigarette ash, or an act of arson by a disgruntled employee – reduced the magnificent building into a pile of twisted metal and ash. The destruction fortified cast iron and glass's reputation for fragility and impermanence. Unlike stone or concrete, common materials for monuments, glass has traditionally not conveyed endurance or permanence; or, in another word, monumentality. Apple's cube is an exceptional glass building, for it relies nearly exclusively on laminated glass for its structure. The cube's public visibility has contributed to glass's acceptance as a suitable material for monuments.

Furthermore, Elliot noted in 1964 that new types of buildings were emerging that were monumental in form – "dignified in manner, permanent in construction, static in form, geometric in shape, and grandiose in scale" – but non-monumental in function. He included in this type office buildings, schools, and family residences.[62] In these buildings, he writes, "the owner feels that the building's importance to him is (or should be) shared with others and he often confuses the corporation with an institution."[63] He further notes that the architect of such buildings eagerly "imbues the building with meaning that it does not come by naturally."[64] The Apple cube is, by its form, symbolism, and technical prowess, a monument. On the one hand, it is a monument on which meanings are imbued by Jobs. On the other hand, its status as a monument is instilled and reinforced by consumers who have been profoundly impacted by the spirit of Apple products. The public has elevated the cube's status to a monument. Unlike other corporate landmarks that with Apple rank as the most photographed places, the cube and Apple products elicit emotional responses from their users; the Rockefeller Center (built by the Standard Oil family) or Times Square (an intersection in front of a newspaper company), may inspire awe because of other reasons such as their impressive height and the high number of people they attract, but they do not trigger emotional response to their products in the way that the Apple cube does to its devices and brand.

Celebration of Impermanence

Apple's products are known for their attention to minimal aesthetics and simplicity. These qualities are echoed in the culture of Japan, which Jobs admired and visited numerous times. Since his first visit to the country in 1974, and through his spiritual advisor, the Buddhist monk Kōbun Otogawa, Jobs continued to be influenced by Japanese aesthetic culture. The meticulous, ceremonial, multilayered packaging of iPhones and the simplicity of a single button in an iPod are a few details that carry similar sensibilities. Moreover, the Japanese belief in the impermanence of all things is inherently tied to their notion of beauty, writes Donald Keene, an American-born Japanese scholar:

> The frailty of human existence, a common theme in life literature throughout the world, has rarely been recognized as the necessary condition of beauty. The Japanese not only knew this, but expressed their preference for varieties of beauty which most conspicuously betrayed their impermanence. Their favorite flower is of course the cherry blossom, precisely because the period of blooming is so poignantly brief and the danger that the flower may scatter even before one has properly seen them is so terribly great.[65]

The transience of cherry blossoms captures the Japanese notion of *mono mo aware*, which translates to "pathos of things."[66] Impermanence, the basis of this sentiment, is a fundamental condition of existence in the Japanese Buddhist tradition; impermanence is not a source of nihilistic despair but a call to the awareness of brief existence. The Apple cube, with its transparent structure and skin, is continually mutable in its appearance. In one moment, it is a dynamic reflector of the traffic on 5th Avenue, while at another moment, it appears to float like a motionless and silent ghost. Whether Jobs was aware of this metaphoric link to mutability is unknown; however, he was aware of the impermanence of the physical products that Apple produced. In an interview, Jobs commented,

> This is a field where one does not write a *Principia* (by Issac Newton) which holds up for two hundred years, or paints a painting that gets looked at for centuries, or builds a church that will be admired and looked at in astonishment for centuries. No, this is a field where one does one's work, and in ten years, it's obsolete, and really will not be usable within ten or twenty years. You can't go back and use an Apple 1 because there is no software for it.[67]

The planned obsolesce of Apple products – made to be used for no more than a decade – is appropriately mirrored in Apple's association with glass. Intrinsically unstable and mercurial, glass captures the fleeting moment of life through the dynamic reflections of its surroundings.

Monument for the Digital Era

Andreas Huyssen, a theorist and historian of German culture, questions whether monuments need to be built at all in a postmodern era in which monuments live as images. He remarks that the artists Christo and Jean-Claude's veiling of the Reichstag in 100,000 square meters of polypropylene, which lasted for a mere 14 days, lives indefinitely through reproduced images in books, posters, digital files, and souvenirs.[68] Similarly, the cube, as one of the most photographed landmarks in New York City and the world (Figure 6.13), lives in a countless number of devices and computers, leaving an enduring virtual mark in the collective memory of this generation. Whether the physical glass cube lasts forever seems less significant. "Memory becomes stone in architecture,"[69] writes Huyssen. The Apple cube suggests that people yearn for architectural monuments even in the digital era, but monuments need not be made in stone. Glass is, symbolically and materially, a reflector of the era in which Apple made its intimate machines in glass. Glass is as mercurial as the images of the surroundings that it reflects and the information it transmits. A mediator between computer devices and humans, glass is apt for a monument symbolizing the age of information.

FIGURE 6.13 People gather around the cube on the GM Building plaza.

Photograph: Peter Aaron (2006)/OTTO.

Notes

1 Tim Bajarin, "Learning This 1 Thing Helped Me Understand Apple's Strategy," *Time*, April 3, 2013, accessed July 1, 2019, http://time.com/4723389/apple-strategy-iphone-ipad-apple-tv/.

2 Le Corbusier, Paul Stirton, and Tim Benton, "Glass, the Fundamental Material of Modern Architecture," *West 86th: A Journal of Decorative Arts, Design History, and Material Culture* 19, no. 2 (Fall–Winter 2012), 297.

3 Partner James O'Callaghan was working for engineering firm Dewhurst Macfarlane & Partners at the time he began collaborating with Apple, and until he co-founded his own firm in 2004. He credits his former employer Tim Macfarlane as a pioneer in the field of structural glass. James O'Callaghan "Glass Challenges: Past, Present, and Future" in Paulo J. da Sousa Cruz, Ed., *Structure and Architecture* (London: Taylor & Francis, 2016), 41.

4 David Crandall, Lars Backstrom, Daniel Huttenlocher, and Jon Kleinberg, "Mapping the World's Photos," *WWW '09 Proceedings of the 18th International Conference on World wide Web in Madrid, Spain* (New York, ACM: 2009), 761–770.

5 Henry Urbach. "Garden of Earthly Delights" in Sabine Schulze and Ina Grätz, Eds.,*Apple Design* (Hamburg: Hatje Cantz, 2011), 107.

6 Isobel Armstrong *Victorian Glassworlds: Glass Culture and the Imagination 1830–1880* (Oxford: Oxford University Press, 2008), 11

7 Rosemarie Haag Bletter, "Interpretation of Glass Dreams: Expressionist Architecture and the History of the Crystal Metaphor," *Journal of the Society of Architectural Historians* 40, no. 1 (March, 1981), 22.

8 Karl Backus, a Principal at Bohlin Cywinski Jackson who has served as the Design Principal for Apple retail stores, invited James O'Callaghan to work on the Apple project following collaboration with BCJ on the Corning Museum. For Corning, the team also worked with TriPyramid Structures, a Massachusetts metal design and fabrication firm that would provide the custom fabricated metal fittings for many of Apple's glass structures. BCJ had mentioned the possibility of an all-glass staircase with Apple prior to O'Callaghan's involvement on the SoHo store. Karl Backus, phone interview by author, August 16, 2019.

9 Katy Devlin, "The Amazing Evolution of Glass at Apple," *Glass Magazine*, accessed June 18, 2018, https://glassmagazine.com/glassblog/amazing-evolution-glass-apple–1513465.

10 O'Callaghan, "Glass Challenges," 45.

11 James O'Callaghan, "Glass Structures and Stairs to Cubes" in Freek Bos, Christian Louter, and Fred Veer, Eds., *Challenging Glass: Conference on Architectural and Structural Applications of Glass, Faculty of Architecture, Delft University of Technology* (Delft: Delft University of Technology, 2008), 30.

12 O'Callaghan, "Glass Structures and Stairs to Cubes," 30.

13 Armstrong, *Victorian Glassworlds* 205.

14 Backus says it is ambiguous whether it was Bohlin who first sketched a cube, or it was Jobs who first suggested the idea of a cube or square, which Jobs considered a pure shape. He recalls they happened nearly simultaneously, suggesting that no single person generated the idea of the cube. Karl Backus, phone interview 2019.

15 William Bostwick, "Apple Store Cube Is More Popular Landmark than Statue of Liberty: Cornell Report," *Fast Company*, March 24, 2010, accessed September 18, 2018, www.fastcompany.com/90182902/apple-store-cube-is-more-popular-land mark-than-statue-of-liberty-cornell-report.

16 O'Callaghan, "Glass Structures and Stairs to Cubes," 32–33.

17 Martin Tamke, Jacob Riiber, and Hauke Jungjohann, "Generated Lamella," *LIFE in: Formation. On Responsive Information and Variations in Architecture: Proceedings of the 30th Annual Conference of the Association for Computer Aided Design in Architecture, ACADIA* (New York: ACADIA, 2010), 342.

18 Noel Y.C., "Apple Store Fifth Avenue Glass Cube Getting Simplified," NYC loves NYC (blog), August 22, 2011, accessed June 20, 2019, https://nyclovesnyc. blogspot.com/2011/08/apple-store-fifth-avenue-glass-cube.html.

19 Stephen R. Ledbetter, Andrew R. Walker, and Alan P. Keiller, "Structural Use of Glass," *Journal of Architectural Engineering* 12, no. 3 (2006), 139. Ionoplast is a clear, tough ionically cross-linked ethylene copolymer.

20 O'Callaghan, ""Glass Challenges," 40–41. O'Callaghan credits British glass engineer Tim Macfarlane, for whom he worked prior to establishing his own firm, for pioneering experimental laminated glass beams in the 1990s with such projects as the Yurakucho Subway Station canopy at the Tokyo Forum by Rafael Vinoly and the Keats Grove structure by Rick Mather.

21 Tanay Warerkar, "Apple Store's Glass Cube on Fifth Avenue is Taking a Sabbatical," *Curbed NYC*, May 9, 2017, accessed June 18, 2019, https://ny.curbed.com/2017/4/20/15369578/apple-glass-cube-fifth-avenue.

22 Benjamin Pattou, application for building permit for construction at 767 5th Avenue, filed March 16, 2017 with New York Department of Buildings, accessed February 16, 2019, http://a810-bisweb.nyc.gov/bisweb/JobsQueryByNumberServ let?requestid=2&passjobnumber=123023799&passdocnumber=01.

23 Zoe Rosenberg, "Apple's Improved Fifth Avenue Store Will Include Glass Cube, More Natural Light," *Curbed NYC*, September 12, 2017, accessed August 10, 2018, https://ny.curbed.com/2017/9/12/16296646/apple-fifth-avenue-expansion-renderings-nyc.

24 Warerkar, "Apple Store's Glass Cube."

25 Michael Mulhern, partner at TriPyramid Structures, fabricator of metal hardware for all three cubes, phone interview by author, August 23, 2019.

26 Aki Ishida, "Metabolic Impermanence: The Nakagin Capsule Tower," *Inflection: The Journal of the Melbourne School of Design* 04 (November 2017), 32–43.

27 O'Callaghan, "Glass Structures and Stairs to Cubes," 32–33.

28 "Glass Stair, Apple SoHo Store, Rebuild," TriPyramid, accessed August 20, 2019, www.tripyramid.com/projects?n=932.

29 James O'Callaghan, email message to author, August 23, 2019.

30 O'Callaghan "Glass Challenges," 43.

31 Devlin "The Amazing Evolution of Glass at Apple"

32 "Glass Stair, Apple SoHo Store, Rebuild."

33 Jolie Lee, "Glass Panel Shatters at Apple's Flagship Store in NY," CNBC, last modified January 23, 2014, accessed July 10, 2018, www.cnbc.com/2014/01/22/giant-apple-glass-panel-shatters-due-to-snowblower.html.

34 "iPhone Screen Repair," Apple, accessed June 26, 2019, https://support.apple.com/iphone/repair/service/screen-replacement.

35 "AppleCare+ Plans for iPhones," Apple, accessed June 26, 2019, https://support.apple.com/applecare/iphone. In addition to the already high price of the device, Apple consumers can pay up to $9.99 a month for AppleCare to protect glass and other parts of the phone.

36 Tim Bajarin, "How Corning's Crash Project for Steve Jobs Helped Define the iPhone," *Fast Company*, accessed November 10, 2017, www.fastcompany.com/40493737/how-cornings-crash-project-for-steve-jobs-helped-define-the-iphone.

37 "How it's Made," Corning, accessed June 26, 2019, www.corning.com/gorilla glass/worldwide/en/technology/how-it-s-made.html.

38 "The Float Process," accessed June 26, 2019, Pilkington, www.pilkington.com/en/global/about/education/the-float-process/the-float-process.

39 "How it Works: Corning's Glass Fusion Process," Corning, accessed June 26, 2019, www.corning.com/worldwide/en/innovation/the-glass-age/science-of-glass/how-it-works-cornings-fusion-process.html.

40 *Encyclopaedia Britannica*, *s.v.* "Pyramids of Giza," accessed June 4, 2019, www.britannica.com/topic/Pyramids-of-Giza.

41 Sigfried Giedion, Josep Lluis Sert and Ferdinand Leger, "Nine Points on Monumentality," in Sigfried Giedion, *Architecture, You, and Me: The Diary of a Development* (Cambridge: Harvard, 1958), 48.

42 *Steve Jobs: The Man in the Machine*. Directed by Alex Gibney. New York: Magnolia Pictures, 2015. www.amazon.com/Steve-Jobs-Man-Machine/dp/B014WH94MQ.

43 *Steve Jobs: The Lost Interview*. Directed by Paul Sen. New York: Magnolia Pictures, 2012.

44 *Steve Jobs: The Man in the Machine*.

45 Urbach, "Garden of Earthly Delights," 112.

46 Giedion, *Architecture, You, and Me*, 50.

47 O'Callaghan "Glass Challenges," 45.

48 Backus, phone interview.

49 Mulhern, phone interview. The glass supplier for the second and the third cube was Sedak of Germany.

50 Bruce Trigger, "Monumental Architecture: A Thermodynamic Explanation of Symbolic Behaviour," *World Archaeology* 22, no. 2, 128.

51 O'Callaghan "Glass Challenges," 46.

52 Vicky Ward, "The Untold Story of How the Apple Store Cube Landed in Midtown," *New York Magazine*, September 28, 2014, accessed May 2, 2019, http://nymag.com/intelligencer/2014/09/story-behind-the-apple-store-cube.html.

53 Ward, "The Untold Story."
54 AppleInsider Staff, "Jobs Wants 32-Foot Glass Cube Following Apple Store Lease," *AppleInsider*, December 05, 2005, accessed May 2, 2019, https://appleinsider.com/articles/05/12/05/jobs_wants_32_foot_glass_cube_following_apple_store_lease.
55 Katie Marsal, "Apple Wins Patent for Steve Jobs-Designed Fifth Ave Glass Cube," *AppleInsider*, August 28, 2014, accessed August 1, 2019, https://appleinsider.com/articles/14/08/28/apple-wins-patent-for-steve-jobs-designed-fifth-ave-glass-cube.
56 Kenneth Frampton, "Maison de Verre," *Perspecta* 12 (1969), 77–109, 111–128.
57 Karl Backus Peter Bohlin, Robert Bridger, Benjamin L. Fay, Ronald Bruce Johnson, James O'Callaghan, and Steve P. Jobs. 2014. Building. US Patent D712,067 S, filed October 15, 2012, and issued August 26, 2014.
58 Joshua Randall, "The Rise of Design Patents: Insights from the Apple v. Samsung Battle," *Lexology*, December 4, 2018, accessed July 25, 2019, www.lexology.com/library/detail.aspx?g=bd796b2e-c0a0-409a-b0f0-ed8570418401.
59 Lewis Mumford, "The Death of the Monument," in Naum Gabo, Ben Nicholson, and Leslie Martin, Eds., *Circle: International Survey of Constructive Art* (London: Faber and Faber, 1937), 263–270.
60 Cecil Elliot, "Monuments and Monumentality," *Journal of Architectural Education* 18, no. 4 (March, 1964), 51–53.
61 Elliot, "Monuments and Monumentality," 52.
62 Elliot, "Monuments and Monumentality," 52.
63 Elliot, "Monuments and Monumentality," 52.
64 Elliot, "Monuments and Monumentality," 52.
65 Donald Keene, "Japanese Aesthetics," *Philosophy East and West* 19, no. 3, (July, 1969), 305.
66 *Stanford Encyclopedia of Philosophy*, s.v. "Japanese Aesthetics: *Mono no aware*," accessed March 3, 2019, https://plato.stanford.edu/entries/japanese-aesthetics/#MonoNoAwarPathThin.
67 *Steve Jobs: The Man in the Machine.*
68 Andreas Huyssen, *Present Pasts: Urban Palimpsests and the Politics of Memory* (Palo Alto, CA: Stanford University Press, 2003), 46–47.
69 Huyssen, *Present Pasts*, 30.

7

QUASI-TRANSPARENCY OF HARPA CONCERT HALL AND CONFERENCE CENTRE

Situated in Iceland's Reykjavik harbor like an iceberg washed ashore, the Harpa Concert Hall and Conference Centre (2011) is animated by play of light on the crystalline, steel and glass polygonal façade (Figure 7.1). The building was collaboratively designed by the Danish architects Henning Larsen, the Icelandic firm Batteríið Architects, and the Icelandic-Danish artist Olafur Eliasson, who led the façade design. Enclosed by glass on all sides, the building has a south-facing foyer facing the city; four concert halls at the center; and backstage areas, a rehearsal hall, offices, and administrative spaces fronting the ocean to the north. During its long winters when the concert halls are most active, the concertgoers' views are oriented towards the illuminated streets and buildings of Reykjavik, with their eyes directed away from the dark, cold ocean.[1] At the front entrance on the south façade, arriving guests are shielded from the blistering northern wind. When the sun shines from near the horizon, which is an extended event at this latitude, Harpa takes on an orange glow. The concert hall turns blue when the sun is at its zenith in the south.[2] The combined effect is at once reminiscent of stained glass windows in a Gothic cathedral and the tensegrity and geodesic structures of Buckminster Fuller.

The glass transparency of Harpa is characterized by the word "quasi," a word used by its designer Olafur Eliasson to describe the façade geometry. Harpa's south façade consists of 823 units of a 12-sided[3] steel and glass modular structure roughly 6.5 feet tall (Figure 7.2).[4] The remaining façades and roof consist of two-dimensional, five- or six-sided section cuts of the volumetric polygon modules.[5] At the base of the south elevation where the front doors are located, a standard insulated glass curtain wall encloses the foyer (Figure 7.3), contrasting the visual complexity of the 12-sided glass and steel modules above, which Eliasson calls the "quasi brick." The choice of word "quasi" emphasizes the

FIGURE 7.1 Like an iceberg washed ashore, Harpa is seen at night across the reflective pools facing the city center.

Photograph: Arterra (2016).

FIGURE 7.2 Full-scale partial mockup of 12-sided steel and glass quasi-brick modules that make up the façade. Each module is about the height of a person.

Studio Olafur Eliasson (2011).

FIGURE 7.3 The rectilinear curtain wall at the base of the south façade accommodates front doors, below the slope of the grand stairs.

Photograph: Author (2018).

physically and metaphysically multifaceted qualities of glass. Eliasson's collaborator, Einar Thorsteinn, had been studying the 12-sided form since 1973. In 1988, Thorsteinn first adapted the word "quasi" from quasicrystals in nature, which are structurally ordered like crystals but without the consistent periodicity.[6] French philosopher Michel Serres writes on the subject of "quasi-object."[7] He defines it as a contract between people, using an example of a ball that is passed between players in a field. In the hands of one player, the ball belongs more to that person. As it is passed and caught by another player, that person becomes more prominent as other players recede. In other words, a quasi-object is relational and changeable. The choice of the word "brick" suggests the construction method with which the façade is built; the unitized modules are stacked like masonry bricks, not suspended (Figure 7.4). This chapter is a study of Harpa's quasi-transparency made possible by the building's specific use of glass. Rising from a particular place and time in history, the quasi-transparency of Harpa can be perceived as relative to a multiplicity of changeable factors, including the position of the viewer, the weather, and the time of day or year.

FIGURE 7.4 The steel "quasi-brick" module frames are stacked, not suspended. Olafur Eliasson and Studio Olafur Eliasson in collaboration with Henning Larsen Architects. Façades of Harpa Reykjavik Concert Hall and Conference Centre 2005–2011.

Photo: Osbjørn Jacobsen, 2010. Commissioned by Portus Group for Reykjavik. © 2005–2011 Olafur Eliasson.

The Work of Olafur Eliasson

The work of artist Olafur Eliasson (b. 1964), while difficult to categorize, concerns "perception, movement, embodied experience, and feelings of self."[8] Born to Icelandic parents living in Denmark, Eliasson spent his childhood immersed in the landscapes and cultures of these two countries, which continue to influence his work. Often using elemental materials such as water, ice, light, and air, his artistic approach shares affinities with the Light and Space artists of 1960s southern California, such as Robert Irwin and James Turrell. His explorations into lightweight structures, mathematics, and the study of forms in nature are akin to and inspired by those of Buckminster Fuller and Frei Otto. Eliasson could rightly be called a quasi-artist, not because he is not an artist but rather because his methods are both scientific and artistic. Decidedly spatial and concerned with one's experience of the world, his work has drawn architects' attention – both admiration and skepticism – for his discipline-defying, dexterous manipulation of materials, light, and the ensuing experience. He works across a range of media, from sculpture, photography, and installations, to film. His output often extends beyond the confines of a gallery, expanding into and engaging architecture and public spaces as impetus and contexts for his work.

Studio Olafur Eliasson in Berlin, where he is currently based, consists of over one hundred multidisciplinary collaborators who range from artists, architects, historians, researchers and technologists to cooks. His approach echoes that of *Gesamtkunstwerk*, or a total work of art, synthesizing multiple art modalities. Harpa's façade is the building and also the artwork. In a traditional concert hall, artwork is placed inside the lobby or hung on the walls. At the New York Metropolitan Opera House, for

FIGURE 7.5 Reflective façade and ceiling serve as the chandelier in the foyer. Photograph: Author (2013).

example, the iconic crystal chandeliers are hung from the ceiling of the entry lobby. By comparison, Harpa's structural façade *is* the chandelier that sparkles with sunlight and electric light (Figure 7.5); the façade integrates art, engineering, and architecture. Like the artist himself, his studio, and their work, Harpa's quasi-transparency shares characteristics that stem from a variety of disciplines and influences.

Icelandic Landscape and Northern Light

As with many of Eliasson's artworks, Harpa's crystalline forms and effects are rooted in geometries and phenomena of the Icelandic landscape. *Moss Wall* (1994), for example, weaves reindeer moss, native to Iceland, into a mesh that covers an entire gallery wall. The faint grayish green moss grows like a vertical carpet, emitting the faint scent of living plants. *Horizon Series* (2002) is a collection of 40 horizon lines, all photographed in Iceland. Eliasson methodically recorded variances in space, weather, and light from different regions. Likewise, an impetus for Harpa's façades is the Icelandic landscape; Harpa is brought to life with metaphors of mineral formations and elemental phenomena – volcanos, basalt rocks, black sand, arctic light, glaciers,

FIGURE 7.6 Harpa's façade is suggestive of Iceland's glacier lagoon.

Photograph: Author (2013).

FIGURE 7.7 The play of light on Harpa's façade is evocative of the aurora borealis, as seen from the Myvatn Hofdi overlook, Iceland.

Photograph: Johnathan Ampersand Esper.

geysers, and lagoons (Figure 7.6). These natural elements become fused with music and the art of storytelling within the intense colored walls of the concert halls and the kaleidoscopic building envelope.

The façade merges basalt column-like shapes with colored light effects of the aurora borealis (Figure 7.7). Although the artist claims that the basalt was not a source of this geometry and instead credits the mathematical studies by his studio,[9] the public associates the geometry of the exterior skin with hexagonal basalt columns commonly found along the coastlines, rivers, and streams of Iceland. Basalt columns form when lava reaches the earth's surface at a volcano. As the lava cools down, it contracts and fractures, forming hexagonal columns.[10] In contrast to the opaque, gray basalt, Harpa's "quasi-brick" envelope is transparent and vibrant. The crystalline foyer enclosed in a variety of reflective, tinted glass starkly contrasts the massif-like cast concrete walls of the concert halls. Inside these dark gray walls are four performance halls with four distinct color schemes: red, purple, silver-gray, and yellow. They reference the four elements of fire, air, water, and earth, which are called, respectively, *Eldborg* (Fire Castle), *Norðurljós* (Northern Lights), *Silfurberg* (Iceland spar, a rare translucent calcite crystal), and *Kaldalón* (Cold Lagoon).[11] The rich colors and textures of the interior material finishes become illuminated by electric light to create spectacles. The main hall, colored in deep hues of red lava for fire, is appropriately named Eldborg, a volcanic crater in Iceland known for its near-perfect form.[12]

Another iconic work of architecture in Reykjavik, the church of Hallgríms-kirkja (1937–1986) by Guðjón Samúelsson, also resembles basalt rock formations (Figure 7.8). Monumental in presence at the top of a hill, it is the tallest building in the country. However, unlike Harpa's crystalline façades, the church is opaque, built with exposed site-cast concrete, echoing the gray skies of long Icelandic

FIGURE 7.8 Hallgrímskirkja church (1937–1986) by Guðjón Samúelsson in Reyjka-vik recalls the geometry of the basalt rocks.

Photograph: Maja Hitij.

winters. The interior is spartan and subdued in gray and white, reflecting Northern European protestant churches or perhaps seemingly echoing the lives spent working in the harsh arctic landscape. In contrast, Harpa combines the static geometry of the basalt rocks with the dynamic, polychrome luminosity of an aurora borealis. Excitation of atmospheric constituents, including oxygen and nitrogen, causes the aurora borealis, which appears as curtain-like, parallel rays of colored light dancing in the sky. Like a magnetic field interacting with charged particles from the sun, Harpa's polyhedral façades reflect and refract light that shifts in color in response to the viewer's position or the change in the weather.

"Both This and That" Glass Architecture

"Quasi" is defined as "apparently but not really; seemingly" and "being partly or almost."[13] It stems from the Latin word quasi, meaning "as if, almost." As Serres defined the quasi-object to be relational and changeable, the quasi-brick could be understood as more one thing, or more something else, depending on its context. As art historian Philip Ursprung asked Eliasson, does quasi-brick imply that the artist intended the glass bricks to be something they are not? The artist replied that it means the brick to be multiple things: "By 'quasi' I mean both the one and the other – both this and that at the same time. This attitude allows for something non-prescribed to emerge ... quasi is concerned with unpredictability."[14] For Harpa, "quasi" not only characterizes the glass brick unit, but also the building as a whole. Harpa itself possesses a "both this and that" transparency with its multifaceted, volumetric façade – a conventional double façade's unorthodox cousin. As the name "brick" suggests, the façade is made by stacking glass and steel modules, more like the nonbearing glass blocks of such buildings as Maison de Verre, except that the steel in Harpa's quasi-bricks is structural. The reference to a masonry material in its name also suggests that this glass façade is not light but heavy, in both appearance and weight, contrary to the aspirations of many modern and contemporary glass buildings.

Qualities of "both this and that" result from the quasi-brick that is simultaneously the skin and the structure. Unlike most glass buildings that rely solely on steel or concrete for structure, the quasi-bricks are mechanically fastened to each other to make a self-supporting polygonal steel frame that also supports the roof. The sides that face the exterior seal out the moisture and air, while the isolated airspace within the quasi-brick units provides insulation against the arctic wind. Whereas a standard insulated glass unit (IGU) air gap is one inch or less, the quasi-brick's air gap is tall enough to accommodate a person inside for maintenance and repair (Figure 7.9).

When seen from the outside on a sunny day, the building appears as a dark gray block of glass. Upon entering the building from the south façade, visitors unexpectedly encounter a bright, kaleidoscopic atrium that soars upward, with expansive views towards the city and the harbor. On the roof (Figure 7.10), moreover, tinted black, hexagonal glass sheets with a metallic coating cover the

FIGURE 7.9 The steel and glass module accommodates a person for cleaning and maintenance.

Photograph: View Pictures (2011).

FIGURE 7.10 Hexagonal glass sheets on the roof reflect the sky.

Photograph: Author (2018).

insulation and the roof membrane; a structural slab sits underneath the glass, so the roof appears entirely opaque. As a result of this opaque backing, the glass behaves like a mirror that reflects the sky. The glass serves no practical function in this location, which is only accessible to invited guests; the architects' design intent was to have a building with glass on all faces, including its fifth – the roof.[15] The exterior skin of Harpa is both opaque and transparent, exhibiting a "both this and that" quality.

A Building as a Kaleidoscope

While much of modern glass architecture attempts to make the glass skin disappear, Harpa exploits and amplifies the reflective nature of glass. The changeability of Harp's quasi-transparency emanates from its inspiration, the kaleidoscope. Scottish physicist Sir David Brewster invented the "philosophical toy" in 1817. Brewster derived the word from the Greek words *kalos*, beautiful; *eidos*, aspect; and *skopein*, to see.[16] The kaleidoscope contained two planes of mirror, placed at 60 degrees to each other and that extend thorough the tube length, with small, loose pieces of colored glass. As the viewer rotated the tube, the moving bits of glass reflected symmetrically in infinite variations (Figures 7.11 and 7.12).

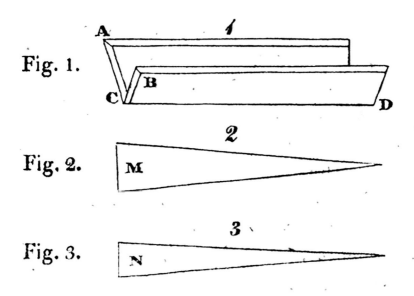

FIGURE 7.11 David Brewster's 1817 patent figure for the kaleidoscope, with the basic configuration of reflecting surfaces in the kaleidoscope. Fig. 2 and Fig. 3 show alternative shapes of the reflectors.

David Brewster, *A Treatise on the Kaleidoscope* (Edinburgh: Archibald Constable & Co., 1819).

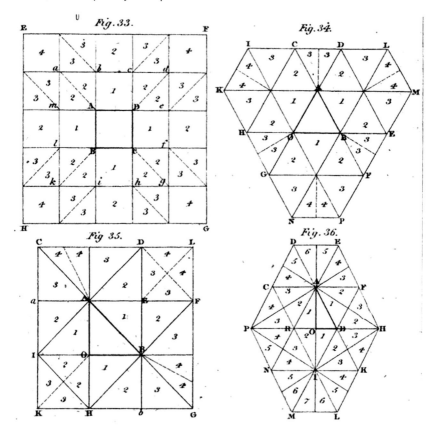

FIGURE 7.12 Diagrams of the patterns of the polycentral kaleidoscope.

David Brewster, A Treatise on the Kaleidoscope (Edinburgh: Archibald Constable & Co., 1819).

Eliasson's body of work includes kaleidoscopic instruments in a variety of scales and configurations, using planes of reflective materials often arranged in increments of 60 degrees. His sculpture *Your compound eye* of 1996 (Figure 7.13) refers to the eyes of arthropods, made up of numerous radially arranged lenses and cones. The artwork consists of six tapering mirrored panels forming a hexagonal kaleidoscope suspended at eye level. Viewers at each end of the scope can see each other in multiple fragmented reflections, not dissimilar to the subtler mirror effects perceived on Harpa's quasi-bricks. Ursprung said in an interview with Eliasson, "Goethe once wrote that telescopes and microscopes make us see the world less clearly. Similarly, rather than sharpening our vision of the world, a kaleidoscope tends to blur it." By this, Goethe meant that scopes obscure the whole of the world of human perception, and blur it by focusing on fragments that make up the whole. To Ursprung's question, Eliasson replied,

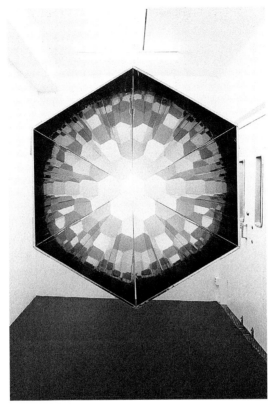

FIGURE 7.13 *Your compound eye* (1996) by Studio Olafur Eliasson. Wood, metal, mirror foil, 90 x 90 x 300 cm. Like eyes of arthropods, the work is made up of numerous radially arranged lenses and cones.

Installation view: Galerie Andreas Brändström, Stockholm, 1996. Photo: Lars Gustavsson. © 1996 Olafur Eliasson.

Our perceptual apparatus is a cultural construction. The way the eye functions is partially a construction, since it processes light from our surroundings, and the brain compresses and digests information around us, but we mistakenly tend to understand these complicated systems as a natural, given thing. The kaleidoscopes play with the fact that what we see can easily be disorganized or reconfigured. They playfully show us multiple ways of seeing the world, so you could say that a kaleidoscope constitutes a different perspective.[17]

Eliasson disrupts the idea that what we see is fixed, but rather that it can easily be destabilized. Art historian Jonathan Crary writes that, for the poet Charles Baudelaire, the kaleidoscope was a machine for "the disintegration of a unitary subjectivity and for the scattering desire into new shifting and labile arrangements, by fragmenting any point of iconicity and disrupting stasis."[18] Similarly, Harpa's quasi-bricks continuously dissolve and reconfigure fragmented views of the city and the interior for the viewer. Moreover, Harpa represents the environment in temporal and dynamic ways. Quasi-bricks turn the transmitted, reflected, and refracted sunlight into theatric colored shadows on the foyer floors and walls. Like a kaleidoscope that dissolves and reorganizes a view with a slight turn of the tube, Harpa's façade alters a perspective of the city with a slight shift in the viewer's body, superimposing the sailboats in the harbor with new hotel buildings and rusted marine warehouses; it shows the world less clearly and blurs its transparency (Figure 7.14).

Furthermore, whereas a kaleidoscope is a construct in a contained view, Harpa's façade is site specific, exposed to sunlight that varies in angles, intensity, and colors. "One of the premises of the design was to 'dematerialize' the building as a static entity,"[19] said Henning Larsen's project partner Peer Telgaard Jeppsen. By dismantling the tube that constitutes the scope, Harpa's façades refuse to repeat a static image and instead show the mutable reflections of its contexts, breaking the relentless symmetry of the self-contained kaleidoscope.

FIGURE 7.14 Full-scale mockup of quasi-bricks dissolves and reorganizes multiple perspectives from the surroundings.

Courtesy of Eignarhaldsfélagið Portus Ltd., Reykjavik, Iceland (2010).

Lightness and Efficiency in Structures by Fuller, Otto, and Thorsteinn

Harpa's quasi-brick and the resulting transparency take influences from the crystalline, faceted surfaces and tensegrity structures of such designers as Buckminster Fuller (Figure 7.15) and Frei Otto. In the 1990s, Eliasson became interested in the provocative ideas and forms of Fuller and Otto.[20] Eliasson says in a 2011 interview: "They (Otto and Fuller) performed a critique of the modern, even while modern was still highly modern."[21] Pioneers in sustainable design, both Otto and Fuller were concerned with appropriate building materials and methods that took cues from nature and left little impact on the earth. Their experiments with lightweight metal frames and cable net structures stemmed from their interests in reducing

FIGURE 7.15 Harpa's quasi-brick took influences from Buckminster Fuller and the geodesic dome.

Photograph: Howard Sochurek/The LIFE Premium Collection/Getty Images (1960).

human footprints, when most modern architects built with heavy steel and concrete structures.

Fuller's Dymaxion structure yields performance with greatest possible efficiency.[22] Fuller showed that the triangle is the geometric plane figure which maximizes rigidity with the least effort. He used an omni-triangulated, omni-symmetric system in his Dymaxion House and geodesic domes since triangles require the least effort to effect.[23] Eliasson's quasi-brick consists of 12 faces, each of which is a hexagon based on 60-degree triangle modules. Frei Otto was also interested in using minimal surfaces to enclose a space. He experimented with soap bubbles, which naturally find the shortest connections between given nodes. He often started his building design with soap bubbles, which later would be modeled in tensioned fabric.[24] The reflective coating on Harpa's façade also calls to mind the multiple colors and reflections in soap bubble surfaces.

Eliasson traces his line of influence to Otto through his longtime collaborator Einar Thorsteinn. An Icelandic engineer, mathematician, and artist, Thorsteinn worked for Otto on the Munich Olympic Stadium (1972) before returning to Iceland, then moved back to Germany where he was hired by Eliasson. Together, they initially experimented with a multitude of prototypical models (Figure 7.16), then developed quasi-bricks specifically for Harpa.

FIGURE 7.16 Installation view at Louisiana Museum of Modern Art, Humlebaek, Denmark, 2014. Olafur Eliasson in collaboration with Einar Thorsteinn. Model room, 2003.

© 2003 Olafur Eliasson and Einar Thorsteinn. Photo: Anders Sune Berg. Moderna Museet.

Eliasson's first artwork to study the quasi-brick was *Quasi Brick Wall* (2002) built of 12-sided clay bricks stacked to 1.6 meters high and 6 meters long.[25] The brick faces are clad in polished stainless steel, which reflects the surrounding trees on the site. The mirrored images of trees blur the perception of the quasi-bricks' solidity. To the viewers, it appears as though they are seeing trees behind the wall, through hollow bricks, when they are really seeing reflections of trees. In 2003, Eliasson completed another project named *Negative Quasi Brick Wall*, which consists of 102 quasi-bricks, each unit folded from one sheet of polished stainless steel. The bricks are hollow and open at both ends, which lets the viewer both see through the wall and see reflections of multidirectional views reflected on the mirrored faces. These projects share characteristics with, and serve as precursors to, Harpa's façade. Quasi-bricks are stacked, self-supporting structures, instruments that show the world layered with reflections of itself.

The glass transparency of Harpa developed from these predecessors' light-weight structures. Eliasson says that he and Thorsteinn had been experimenting with the polyhedron in architecture, "without compromising the project's ethical message," in works by Otto and Fuller; their lightweight structures were synonymous with efficiency and low material costs.[26] Otto's research into efficient structures in nature had a fundamental proposition; lightweight construction – doing more with less – is congruent with concerns over depletion of nonrenewable resources and disruptions to sensitive ecological systems.[27] However, efficiency in form inspired by biology had a paradoxical problem. Otto and his office dedicated an intense amount of time to finding forms that minimized material weight. Otto's team spent 20,000 man-hours designing the Montreal Pavilion (1967), while it took just three and a half weeks to erect on site.[28]

Similarly, Thorsteinn and Eliasson spent many years predating the concert hall to study polyhedron geometries, before applying the knowledge to Harpa's self-supporting quasi-brick. Eliasson worked with contractors to build full-scale prototypes, testing the reflective qualities of glass and refining metal joint details. Contractors were hesitant to take responsibility for a complex façade that had never been used as a building envelope. Only a builder in China was willing to take the risk, but not without complications.[29] One of the five façade subcontractors had failed to follow the architects' specifications for cast-iron corner nodes. The metal parts for the south façade had already been delivered from China to Reykjavik and assembled on site when this error was discovered. The contractors had to dismantle the façade and rebuild it with the corrected parts. Instead of choosing a readily tested and available curtain wall system, building with a previously untested system at a scale this large quickly proved to be costly and inefficient. Moreover, due to the pioneering nature of the façade design, local fabricators could not provide the metal components, which had to be shipped from China. It was difficult to argue for the efficiency of Harpa's façade during its design and construction. The finished façade possesses, however, aspects of efficiency advocated by Otto

FIGURE 7.17 Structural quasi-brick façade on the left meets the non-structural curtain wall on the right, supported by columns.

Photograph: Author (2018).

and Fuller. The quasi-brick, serving both as the skin and the structure, removes the hierarchy of conventional curtain walls in which glass plates are suspended from structural floors and columns. This contrast is most evident in building corners where the quasi-bricks of the south façade meet the other curtain wall types (Figure 7.17). On the south façade, where the glass becomes most animated with daylight, Harpa's polyhedral steel and glass façade stands unobstructed by columns, foregrounding its kaleidoscopic effects.

For an arctic country of Iceland to build an all-glass building as a national symbol may appear unsustainable at first glance. It appears to contradict Eliasson's interest in Fuller and Otto's ethical message. However, Iceland's abundant geothermal resources enable this seemingly unlikely choice of material. In 2015, nine out of every ten houses in the country were heated directly with geothermal energy.[30] Iceland's widespread use of renewable energies is relatively new. Until the introduction of imported oil in the 20th century, the majority of Icelandic homes were heated using animal body heat, and by the burning of coal, peat, and sheep dung.[31] After World War II until the oil crisis of the 1980s, Iceland was dependent on foreign oil.[32] Today, nearly 100% of the electricity consumed by the country comes from renewable energy. Harpa in all glass would have been prohibitively expensive to heat without geothermal energy. Only with the relatively inexpensive cost of heating in Iceland, is this crystalline building sensible. In other words, the building's application of glass is particular to its place and time in history.

Ten Reflective Glass Types, Infinite Light Patterns

Harpa's kaleidoscopic effects result from a careful orchestration of different glass types with a microscopically thin layer of chemical coating that alters the behavior of light. Harpa's four façades use ten different types of glass, varying in colors and reflectivity (Figure 7.18).[33] Two of the types are a standard clear class and an anti-reflective glass. The latter has a coating that reduces unwanted reflection, with a reflectivity rate of 1% instead of 8% on standard float glass.[34] Antireflective glass is often specified for panorama windows and display cases; it maximizes light transmission and the see-through effect. Additionally, Harpa contains five different types of reflective glass, each with a varying color tint or a degree of reflectivity. Last, there are three types of dichroic glass, which have thin layers of high and low refraction metal oxide coatings that transmit certain colors of light while refracting others.[35] The three types used in Harpa transmit the colors of yellow, green, and orange, and refract the colors of blue, red, and purple, respectively.[36] Like the colored glass chips in a kaleidoscope, dichroic glass immersed in light scatters an array of colored shadows (Figure 7.19).

Eliasson's studio combined these ten different types of glass in a painterly manner across the southern quasi-brick façade, resulting in variations of colors, reflectivity, and transparency. When the antireflective glass is paired with clear glass, for instance, the viewer sees straight through the brick; whereas when it is paired with a dichroic glass, one sees kaleidoscopic reflections of the interior,

FIGURE 7.18 On the south façade, the orange, purple, and green colors of dichroic glass are seen overlapping both themselves and the varying colors of the sky.

Photograph: Nicholas Coates (2016).

FIGURE 7.19 Colors of various types of glass and shadows of steel frames projected on the foyer stairs.

Photograph: Author (2013).

FIGURE 7.20 Under certain angles and light conditions, the density of the steel frames dominates over the presence of the glass.

Photograph: Author (2018).

washed with two different colors of light that vary with the viewing angle. Furthermore, the design team studied the effects of sun angles on transparency and colors.[37] The bricks appear solid and opaque in the morning sun, as the cityscape and the dark ocean are seen reflected on the glass surfaces. Conversely, the glass cladding on the bricks appears to disappear under certain sun angles, drawing attention to the skeletal metal frames instead of the glass (Figure 7.20).

The consequent light and shadow play is characteristically Nordic. The northern sun differs from that of the Mediterranean south, where sunlight shines from directly above and produces sharp, crisp shadows. Christian Norberg-Schulz writes that the north is distinguished from the south by its light: "Here in the North, the sun does not rise to the zenith but grazes things obliquely and dissolves in an interplay of light and shadow."[38] He characterizes the Nordic light as having a mood: "In the North we occupy a world of moods, or shifting nuances, of never-resting forces, even when the light is withdrawn and filtered through an overcast sky."[39] Harpa's façade is an instrument that amplifies the "northern mood" through a play of light. As sunlight shines obliquely, the quasi-brick façades project blurred shadows and light filtered by fluctuating weathers. The floors and walls of the foyer capture subtle shifts in mood as the sun moves in and out of the clouds' shadows.

The play of colored light in glass architecture may be traced back to the work of poet Paul Scheerbart and his architect friend Bruno Taut. While Eliasson studied art as a college student in the 1990s, post-modernism was coming to pass. In researching alternative critiques of the modern, Eliasson explored the works of Taut, Scheerbart, and their kaleidoscopic cities of the 1910s.[40] Taut and Scheerbart depicted their fantastic premonitions of glass architecture in words and drawings, and prototyped their ideas in Taut's Cologne Glass Pavilion of 1914. Scheerbart, an author of fiction, wrote a technical book advocating double-wall colored glass and metal frame architecture. Taut asked Scheerbart to write 14 mottos that would be incised at the 14-sided base of the building. The rhyming mottos, intended to celebrate and promote the material of glass, included "Coloured glass destroys hatred," and "Bricks may crumble. Coloured glass endures."[41] Visitors stepped down the stairs that flanked cascading water lit from the bottom of a water basin. At the base of the stairs, they entered the "kaleidoscope room" where colored light were projected on a screen.[42] The Pavilion not only impressed visitors with dazzling effects of light and glass but also with the glass manufacturers' latest glass technology. The main sponsor of the building, German Luxfer Prism Syndikat, provided the 4-inch square prismatic glass tiles for the inside layer of the double-layered glass dome.[43] Luxfer tiles had a light-refracting, ridged profile designed to direct light deeper into a building and to project light onto walls and ceilings instead of onto floors. In Harpa, Eliasson materializes buildings depicted as polychrome glass glaciers, mountains, and flowers in Taut's drawings (Figure 7.21). While Harpa's quasi-bricks have the appearance of prisms, they do not reflect and refract light the way the ridged prisms of Taut's Pavilion did. The quasi-brick's glass is coated with microscopically thin chemical layers that transmit light and refract light, but the thinness of the glass does not allow it to bend light

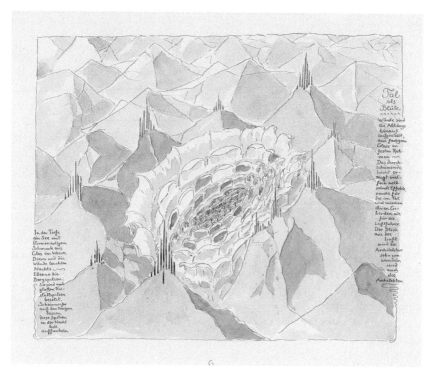

FIGURE 7.21 A drawing from the book *Alpine Architecture* by Bruno Taut. The valley is transformed into a flower made of glass which glows at night.

Akademie der Künste, Berlin, Alpine Architektur aus dem Bruno-Taut-Archiv Nr. 9.

and redirect it as a Luxfer prism does. In this way, quasi-brick is only prismatic and not truly a prism.

Scheerbart's writings on glass architecture parallel Harpa's façades, not only in their references to colored glass and the effects of light but also in the symbolism ascribed to architecture. The name Harpa holds a symbolic significance for Iceland. It is not only the name of a musical instrument but also the first month of spring in Iceland.[44] Appropriately, Harpa stands for optimism after a long and dark Icelandic winter. Moreover, it holds a particular importance in the recent history of Iceland. Harpa's design started in 2007, came to a halt in 2008 with the devastating bankruptcy of Iceland's three largest lenders,[45] recovered with Iceland's economic rise, and suffered embarrassing publicity from a volcano eruption in 2010.[46] Construction was finally completed in 2011 just as Iceland began recovering economically.[47] As a result of these national disasters, the mythological, symbolic value of Harpa grew in importance beyond the architects' initial intentions or the fulfilment of practical functions. Art historian Rosemarie Haag Bletter writes that in Scheerbart's work, crystal and glass, which he uses interchangeably, are a metaphor for individual transcendence.[48] His descriptions of mobile glass houses, floating structures, and constantly changing electric light amplified by reflections on water and glass are all symbolic of transformation. She goes on to say that this mutability of glass in his writing stands for the metamorphosis of society. In this light, a crystalline concert hall on the harbor is an apt symbol of Iceland's collective transformation from bankruptcy to recovery.

Both Taut and Eliasson created a kaleidoscopic spectacle not only with daylight but also with colored electric light projected between glass sheets. Taut placed electric light with colored filters inside the double façade in the Glass Pavilion in Cologne. Nearly a century later, Eliasson developed strip customizable color LEDs that project light inside the steel and glass quasi-bricks.

Electric Effects

Situated just south of the Arctic Circle, Reykjavik possesses unusual daylight conditions. In December, there are only about five hours of limited daylight from 11 am to 4 pm and the sun barely rises above the horizon. During Iceland's winter, commuters encounter Harpa primarily in the dark, or in a low, soft light. Since Harpa's façades incorporate over 700 RGB LED strips, they stay luminous in the dark days of Reykjavik winters (Figure 7.22). Each strip, roughly 4.5 feet long, is

FIGURE 7.22 Harpa's façades incorporate over 700 RGB LED strips and illuminate Reykjavik through long winter nights.

Photograph: Al Robinson.

housed in a slim, custom-fabricated aluminum extrusion.[49] The fixture incorporates light diffusers and lenses that aim the light outward, away from the people inside. The nuanced, diffused light is seen indirectly by viewers, and the fixtures themselves are kept concealed within the void of quasi-brick. Each strip is programmed independently on a 75-second loop, with staggered starting times, emitting a full spectrum of colors.

The effect closely mirrors Scheerbart's written descriptions. In his book *Glasarchitecktur* of 1914, he describes double glass façades illuminated from within: "With this type of lighting the whole glass house becomes a big lantern which, on peaceful summer and winter nights, shines like fire-flies and glow-worms."[50] The fluctuating colors of Harpa's glass, combining natural and artificial light, are endlessly varied and dynamic throughout the day and the year. In addition to the changing LED colors, the artificial light interacts differently with each of the glazing types, amplifying the kaleidoscopic effect of infinitely variable light conditions.

Temporal Transparency

Harpa, as with Eliasson's other artwork, demands appreciation over a period of time. He says, in an interview about his work *The Weather Project* (2003) at the Tate Modern's Turbine Hall, that beauty in his projects is understood individually, as each person takes time to immerse themselves in the space:

> the quality of the experience really depends on the combined performativity of the installation and the person; if the situation allows for a very individual experience, I'm not afraid of the work being called "beautiful"… "Beauty" is a very complex term: one version of it tends to create a discrepancy between where you think you are and where you actually are, whereas another version is more generous, in a way, since it creates an overlap between where you think you are and where you are in fact.[51]

He compares the former type of beauty to those that are standardized, such as what a Marlborough cigarette advertisement portrays, which "ages very quickly" because it is intended to be read in only one way.[52] Eliasson's work asks to be understood individually over an extended period of time. With *The Weather Project*, for example, the light from the artificial sun shone from the top while the mist machines streamed fog into the atmosphere, diffusing the light from the sun into the space. Basked in this intense yellow light, the museum visitors lay on their backs to view their own reflections on the mirrored ceiling above.[53] Similar to *The Weather Project*, which prompted multiple mutable readings over time, incorporation of time is central to understanding Harpa's transparency. Harpa's façades function as windows and as lamps.

The studio has explored, through multiple quasi-brick projects, how the bricks can be stacked differently to produce varying effects over time. The quasi-bricks at Harpa are physically fixed, but their transparency effects are dynamic and temporal. In Iceland, the light ranges from the midnight sun in the summer months to the long arctic nights in the winter when there are only a few hours of sun each day; Harpa's transparency is relative to its unique diurnal and seasonal cycle.

An Instrument for Seeing

Like Eliasson's other works of art, Harpa is an instrument for viewers in motion to perceive the dynamic world. Eliasson often titles his work with possessive pronouns, such as *Your solar attention*, *Your rainbow panorama*, or *Your intuition*. His environments, as the titles suggest, call into question the certainty of one's perception of the world, often by creating, blurring, and multiplying reflections. Harpa's quasi-brick façade is an instrument for seeing collectively. Unlike his museum installations, in which the viewer's position is relatively fixed, with his kaleidoscopes, viewers are dispersed and moving throughout the building. Their reflections are seen together with those of others seeing themselves seeing. Superimposed on the mobile reflections of the viewers are fragmented views of Reykjavik harbor, in motion and illuminated in mutable arctic light. Harpa's quasi-transparent glass is at once clear and obstructed. The world is seen, but blurred.

Notes

1 Alexandra Onderwater, "Let There Be Light," *Mark: Another Architecture* no. 35 (2011 December, 2011/ January, 2012), 111.
2 Onderwater, "Let There Be Light," 111.
3 In Plato's book *Timaeus*, he included dodecahedron, or a 12-sided polyhedron, as one of five cosmic solids, each associated with one of five elements. Dodecahedron was associated with heavenly matter. Eliasson does not mention this link to Plato's polyhedral. See Judith V. Field, "Rediscovering the Archimedean Polyhedra: Piero della Francesca, Luca Pacioli, Leonardo da Vinci, Albrecht Dürer, Daniele Barbaro, and Johannes Kepler," *Archive for History of Exact Sciences* 50, no. 3/4 (September, 1997), 241–289.
4 Caia Hagel, "Harpa-Reykjavic Concert Hall and Conference Center," *Architect*, October 6, 2011, accessed May 24, 2019, www.architectmagazine.com/design/buildings/harpareykjavik-concert-hall-and-conference-centre_o.
5 "Henning Larsen Architects, Harpa Concert Hall and Conference Centre, Reykjavik, Iceland 2007–2011," *A + U: Architecture and Urbanism* 9492 (September, 2011), 37.
6 *Encyclopedia Brittanica*, s.v. "quasicrystal,"accessed June 5, 2019, www.britannica.com/science/quasicrystal.
7 Michele Serres, "Theory of the Quasi-Object," in *Serres, Parasite* (Minneapolis, MN: University of Minnesota Press, 2007), 224–234.
8 "Biography," Olafur Eliasson, accessed April 24, 2019, https://olafureliasson.net/biography.
9 Haukur S. Magnússon, "Is Harpa Just a Façade: The House Olafur Eliasson Built," *Reykjavik Grapevine*, May 6, 2011, accessed April 4, 2019, https://grapevine.is/mag/feature/2011/05/06/is-harpa-just-a-facade/.

10 Evelyne Mervine, "Geology Word of the Week: C is for Columnar Jointing," *American Geophysical Union* (blog), November 18, 2012, accessed April 4, 2019, https://blogs.agu.org/georneys/2012/11/18/geology-word-of-the-week-c-is-for-columnar-jointing/.

11 Magnússon, "Is Harpa Just a Façade."

12 "Harpa Concert Hall and Conference Center," Henning Larsen, accessed April 30, 2019, https://henninglarsen.com/en/projects/featured/0676-harpa-concert-hall-and-conference-center/.

13 *Oxford English Dictionary*, s.v. "Quasi," accessed June 1, 2019, https://en.oxforddictionaries.com/definition/quasi.

14 Philip Ursprung, *Studio Olafur Eliasson: An Encyclopedia* (Cologne: Taschen, 2016), 333.

15 Sigurður Einarsson of Batteríið Architects, interview by author, Reykjavik, May 31, 2018.

16 Klaus-Dieter Graf and Bernard R. Hodgson, "Popularizing Geometrical Concepts: The Case of the Kaleidoscope," *For the Learning of Mathematics* 10, no. 3 (November, 1990), 42.

17 Ursprung, *Studio Olafur Eliasson*, 239.

18 Jonathan Crary, *Techniques of the Observer: On Vision and Modernity in the Nineteenth Century* (Cambridge, MA: MIT Press, 1990), 113–114.

19 Peer Telgaard Jeppsen quoted in Onderwater, "Let There Be Light," 108.

20 Joseph Grima and Olufar Eliasson, "Eliasson's Kaleidoscope," *Domus* no. 950 (2011), 30–32.

21 Grima and Eliasson, "Eliasson's Kaleidoscope," 30.

22 R. Buckminster Fuller and Robert Marks, *Dymaxion World of Buckminster Fuller* (Garden City, NY: Doubleday, 1960), 4.

23 Fuller and Marks, *Dymaxion World*, 43.

24 Ian Liddell, "Frei Otto and the Development of Gridshells," *Case Studies in Structural Engineering* 4 (2015) 39–49.

25 Ursprung, *Studio Olafur Eliasson*, 338–339.

26 Grima and Eliasson, "Eliasson's Kaleidoscope," 30–32.

27 Philip Drew, *Frei Otto: Form and Structure* (London: Crosby Lockwood Staples, 1976), 12.

28 Drew, *Frei Otto*, 12.

29 Magnússon"Is Harpa Just a Façade."

30 Halla Hrund Logadóttir, "Iceland's Sustainable Energy Story: A Model for the World?" *UN Chronicle*, December, 2015, accessed March 2, 2019, https://unchronicle.un.org/article/iceland-s-sustainable-energy-story-model-world.

31 Björnsson, Sveinbjörned, *Geothermal Development and Research in Iceland* (Reykjavik: Orkustofnun, 2010), 14, www.nea.is/media/utgafa/GD_loka.pdf.

32 Björnsson, *Geothermal Development*, 15.

33 Hagel "Harpa-Reykjavic Concert Hall."

34 "Schott Amiran®: Anti-Reflective Glass for Façades," Schott, accessed January 15, 2019, www.us.schott.com/architecture/english/products/anti-reflective-glass/amiran.html.

35 Artist James Carpenter and his studio James Carpenter Design Associates have explored architectural uses of dichroic glass in public art and building projects since the late 1970s. See Sandro Marpillero, *James Carpenter: Environmental Refractions* (New York: Princeton Architectural Press, 2006).

36 Hagel "Harpa-Reykjavic Concert Hall."

37 Hagel "Harpa-Reykjavic Concert Hall."

38 Christian Norberg-Schulz, *Nightlands: Nordic Buildings* (Cambridge, MA: MIT Press, 1996), 2.

39 Norberg-Schulz, *Nightlands,* 3.

40 Grima and Eliasson, "Eliasson's Kaleidoscope," 32.

41 Dennis Sharp, "Introduction," *Paul Scheerbart and Bruno Taut, Glass Architecture, by Paul Scheerbart; and Alpine Architecture, by Bruno Taut ed.* (New York: Praeger, 1972), 14.

42 Rosemarie Haag Bletter, "The Interpretation of the Glass Dream: Expressionist Architecture and the History of the Crystal Metaphor," *Journal of the the Society of Architectural Historians* 40, no. 1 (March, 1981), 34.

43 Dietrich Neumann, "The Century's Triumph in Lighting: The Luxfer Prism Companies and Their Contribution to Early Modern Architecture," *Journal of the Society of Architectural Historians* 54, no. 1 (March, 1995), 24–53. Luxfer prisms were used in early skyscrapers in Chicago, such as the Chicago Stock Exchange (1923) by Louis Sullivan and the Home Insurance Building (1885, retrofitted with Luxfer prisms in 1895) by William Le Baron Jenny.

44 Onderwater, "Let There Be Light," 104.

45 Simon Bowers, "Iceland Banking Collapse: Diary of a Death Spiral," *The Guardian*, June 26, 2012, accessed August 30, 2019, www.theguardian.com/business/2012/jun/26/iceland-banking-collapse-diary-death-spiral. Resulted in loss of combined assets ten times the size of the country's economy.

46 In 2010, one of the largest volcanoes in Iceland, Eyjafjallajökull, had a relatively modest eruption that, due to the prevailing weather, resulted in an out-of-proportion ash dispersal across transatlantic flight paths. The ashes paralyzed 300 airports in about two dozen countries for six days. Airlines lost $1.7 billion in missed revenues.

47 Harpa was the first and most visible building of the East Harbour Project (*Austurhofn*), a nearly 680,000-square-foot mixed-use redevelopment of Reykjavik harbor, designed to enhance connections between the city center and the old harbor. See Hagel "Harpa-Reykjavic Concert Hall."

48 Bletter, "The Interpretation of the Glass Dream," 32–33.

49 "Harpa: Reykjavik's New Concert Hall, Emotional and Full of Energy, Like Iceland Itself," Zumtobel press release, December, 2011, accessed May 1, 2019, www.zumtobel.com/media/downloads/Pressinformation-ZT_Harpa_ConcertHall_EN.pdf. Custom fixtures were made by the Austrian lighting manufacturer Zumtobel.

50 Sharp, *Paul Scheerbart and Bruno Taut*, 51.

51 Ursprung, *Studio Olafur Eliasson*, 75

52 Ursprung, *Studio Olafur Eliasson*, 75

53 Ursprung, *Studio Olafur Eliasson*, 17.

INDEX

Page numbers in *italics* refer to figures or images.

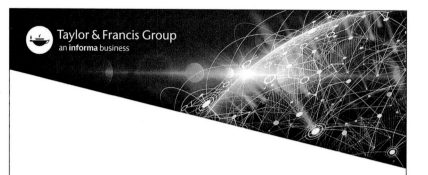

Taylor & Francis Group
an **informa** business

Taylor & Francis eBooks

www.taylorfrancis.com

A single destination for eBooks from Taylor & Francis
with increased functionality and an improved user
experience to meet the needs of our customers.

90,000+ eBooks of award-winning academic content in
Humanities, Social Science, Science, Technology, Engineering,
and Medical written by a global network of editors and authors.

TAYLOR & FRANCIS EBOOKS OFFERS:

A streamlined
experience for
our library
customers

A single point
of discovery
for all of our
eBook content

Improved
search and
discovery of
content at both
book and
chapter level

REQUEST A FREE TRIAL
support@taylorfrancis.com

 Routledge
Taylor & Francis Group

 CRC Press
Taylor & Francis Group